PRAISE F[...]
When Love Sticks [...]

"*When Love Sticks Around* is an instantly engaging memoir that deals with the highs and lows of coming-of-age and the realities and complexities of adulthood. Dayney moves seamlessly through her life from birth, right up to the first moment of motherhood, before losing her own mother to cancer. Her vignettes of life's journeys instantly transport readers into a world unique to her. It's the complexities of the relationships within the pages of her debut novel that are both delightful and also heartbreaking. From the very first page, she has written a book worth sticking around for."

—Donna-Louise Bishop, community life correspondent for *The Eastern Daily Press*, Norfolk, UK

"Ms. Dayney's story of growing up on the wrong side of the tracks in Toledo, Ohio, is a tale of disappointment, grit, and ultimately, love. In her quest to unravel her family's thorny relationships, she brings readers into a cigarette-and-beer-filled world they will not want to leave."

—Amy Francis Dechary, editor of the *Beach Reads* anthology series and president of Third Street Writers

"Each short essay in *When Love Sticks Around* is a marvelous example of the struggles we face throughout our lives, how love in all of its various forms presides through it, and ultimately how together we face both the tragedies and the moments of celebration. Whether the topic is growing up poor, struggling to gain a relationship with a parent, dating, having not-the-best jobs, transitioning into being an adult, or navigating racism, Dayney's mesmerizing narratives and skill at storytelling aid in exploring the complexities of life, all told in simple, relatable ways. Through these candid glimpses of her own experiences, this coming-of-age memoir reaches beyond the moments of growing up to create a visceral testament to all that we love and search for."

—Chelsey Clammer, author of *Circadian* and *BodyHome*

"In *When Love Sticks Around*, Dayney instantly transports us to moments throughout her life with relatable cultural touchstones and references, linking us to her younger self, growing up in a struggling, working-class family in upstate Ohio throughout the 80s and 90s. Her story of family, hope, and perseverance opens a space for us to laugh, acknowledge, and remember moments in life that shape us as adults. It is a work of great compassion and great joy."

—A.E. Bayne, writer, artist, and publisher of *The Fredericksburg Literary and Art Review*

More praise for *When Love Sticks Around*

"Dayney's well-written and poignant collection of personal essays makes you laugh, seethe, and cry. In other words, this is life itself."

—Betsy Ashton, author of *Out of the Desert*

"In a voice as familiar as a life-long friend's and in astonishingly evocative detail, Danielle Dayney charts her journey from a childhood in Toledo, Ohio, longing for love enough to fill an inexplicable emptiness left by her absent father, through the universally awkward teen years and floundering young adulthood, to her life in Brooklyn as a wife, mother, and writer, who discovers through tragedy and triumph that her indomitable mother, steadfast step-father, championing husband, and darling daughter have filled her heart to overflowing. *When Love Sticks Around* will break your heart and then restore it, like a shattered seashell that still sounds like the ocean with just a little bit of glue and a lot of love."

—Elane Johnson, Gotham Writers Workshop

"*When Love Sticks Around* is a compelling and honest portrayal of Danielle Dayney's childhood and relationships. From the beginnings of her parents' relationship to its eventual end, to the introduction of her stepfather, the birth of her sister, the comings and goings of her biological father, and her own marriage, Danielle examines the meaning and the shape of family. The role of father is carefully dissected, and the two men who compete for that role in her life are thoughtfully, subtly contrasted. There is no overt comparison, no stark listing of attributes. Instead, by showing these men and their actions, the reader is led to decide which of them better fulfilled the role. All the relationships in this memoir are viewed with a keen eye and a refreshing sincerity. There is no harsh judgement of anyone, and their actions are described in an almost matter-of-fact tone, leaving the reader feeling a level of inevitability to those actions. The author also doesn't pull punches when examining her own behaviors or feelings. By the end of the narrative, the reader is left with an overwhelming feeling that the author has come to accept that the various events and relationships in her life have shaped her into the person she currently is. There is a great sense of peace in that."

—Asha Rajan, managing editor at *Dead Housekeeping*
and contributing editor at *YeahWrite*

DANIELLE DAYNEY

WHEN *love* STICKS AROUND

BELLE ISLE BOOKS
www.belleislebooks.com

This is a work of creative nonfiction. Though I have changed the names of some individuals to protect their anonymity, and I have in some cases condensed time for storytelling purposes, I have done my best to recreate each story. But please remember that memoirs are based on memory, which is often imperfect.

Copyright © 2022 by Danielle Dayney

No part of this book may be reproduced in any form or by any electronic or mechanical means, or the facilitation thereof, including information storage and retrieval systems, without permission in writing from the publisher, except in the case of brief quotations published in articles and reviews. Any educational institution wishing to photocopy part or all of the work for classroom use, or individual researchers who would like to obtain permission to reprint the work for educational purposes, should contact the publisher

ISBN: 978-1-953021-19-9
LCCN: 2021915132

Author headshot (p. 149) by Kerry Renee Photography
Cover designed by Simpatico Design Studio, LLC
Project managed by Mary-Peyton Crook

Printed in the United States of America

Published by
Belle Isle Books (an imprint of Brandylane Publishers, Inc.)
5 S. 1st Street
Richmond, Virginia 23219

BELLE ISLE BOOKS
www.belleislebooks.com

belleislebooks.com | brandylanepublishers.com

I dedicate this book to my mother,
whom I lost to cancer in 2012.
Because of her, I learned to let go of the
things that are out of my control.

This book is also dedicated to
my husband and two beautiful daughters,
who give me new reasons to hold on each day.

What's in a Name?

My biological father, Don, spent most of the seventies and eighties spinning records in Toledo, Ohio, at a local hot spot called Renee's. He thought he would become famous for his ability to spin records.

One night in the late seventies, Mom asked her cousin, Beatrice, to go out for a night of dancing. Mom and Beatrice hot-rolled their shoulder-length, feathered hair and slipped into dresses like Elvira Hancock's from *Scarface*. Once ready, Mom drove her new Plymouth Barracuda to the south side of town.

They met Don for the first time between his sets. Mom liked that he was a disc jockey, so she approached him at the bar to introduce herself. He liked that she made her own money working as a beautician.

After Don strutted back to the DJ booth, Beatrice said, "He's not even your type. Not even good looking." From photos, I know Don was thin with inky hair like mine, blue eyes, and crooked teeth.

"I know, but there's something about him," said Mom. She liked his smooth swagger.

Don asked her on a date later that night, and Mom said yes.

Mom and Don struggled financially and fought passionately through the early part of their relationship, but she stuck it out with him. She thought she could change him. She gave him every dollar he asked for to support his developing DJ career, and gave up time with friends and family to be only with Don. Mom wanted to stand by him like a "good girlfriend" however she could, and he was eager to be successful, no matter the cost.

Mom cut and styled hair in the Lasalle salon downtown, and she was good at pinching pennies when she needed to. But their money ran low. "I'll sell my car and home if that will help," she offered. Aside from her new car, Mom also owned a trailer home, all at twenty-one.

Don didn't oppose. They sold both and moved into a small and rundown but functional apartment between downtown and the highway.

I don't know the story of how he proposed, but after they'd been dating for one year, he put a simple diamond on her finger. They worked out plans for a magnificent outdoor wedding, complete with a floor-length mermaid-cut lace gown and powder blue polyester suits.

Not long after the wedding, I was conceived.

My first name, Danielle, was chosen by my father. At the time, his best friend—and his best man at the wedding—was a man named Daniel. I don't recall ever meeting Daniel; he was just Don's buddy. They probably met at the disco, which is also where my middle name, Renee, came from. Don picked my middle name too. Mom liked it because it sounded French, reminding her of our ancestors from Quebec.

"She has to be named after my mom too," Mom said. "She'll have a second middle name: Ruth."

After Mom delivered me, Don started working more nights as a DJ. Maybe his initial intentions were good. Maybe he wanted to bring home extra money to keep the itsy-bitsy roof over our heads. But he ended up getting drunk most nights, spending his evenings with girls hanging on him even though a gold wedding ring encircled his finger. Usually, he crawled into bed reeking of alcohol after the sun had already crept up over the horizon.

Night after night, Don worked at Renee's and left Mom in the rundown apartment, raising a child on her own. She was too proud to ask for help and too scared to call it quits and leave. But after my first birthday, when Don drained two thousand dollars in one day from her personal bank account for new records without asking, Mom had finally had enough. She realized that he wasn't going to change. So she packed our bags while Don was at Renee's. Grandpa picked us up and took us home to Lagrange Street, where Mom had grown up. She had no money, no furniture, no husband—just me: Danielle Renee Ruth. She promised to give me the best life she could.

Space Heater

I stood at the top of the steps, twelve stairs and three rooms away from Mom. First: the family room. It seemed so big because I was so small. Even though I was upstairs, I could picture the country blue couch pressed against the wall beneath the window. Our twenty-four-inch television had gone to sleep for the night, and Gizzie, our little dog, snored in a ball somewhere on the braided oval rug. I was supposed to be sleeping too.

I heard laughter, stifled by walls and distance. Why did the adults always have more fun when I was asleep? It wasn't fair. I ran down the stairs, and rough carpet scratched the bottoms of my feet.

When I reached the bottom step, I jumped off and landed on both feet in the living room, then kept running. My gray reflection whizzed past the mirror hanging by the front door. I was so fast!

The next small room contained the big dining table and high-backed chairs with hand-carved curls etched in them. We never ate in the dining room, but I liked to trace my fingers along the detailed chairs, wondering how all the squiggles got pressed into the wood.

Mom must have been perming my aunt's hair. The smell of chemicals drifted from the breakfast nook in the kitchen to the dining room to sting my nose and burn my eyes. Lately, Mom did the family's hair at home. She and her boyfriend, Jim, needed the extra money for our new house. Jim was an okay stepdad, but he already had two kids with another lady.

I still saw my real dad sometimes. At his apartment, in the corner of an empty bedroom with pale blue carpet, sat a small, wooden rocking chair. There were no other toys. One night every other weekend, I'd rock in that chair, clinging to my soft Smurf blanket and the smell of home, thinking of how much I missed Mom. I'd stare at the dead grass and the bit of sidewalk outside the window, wishing Don would take me out there on my trike. For a few years it was like this: one night every other weekend with my dad, but alone. I preferred the drafty house with Mom and Jim.

Cool air whisked across my bare arms, giving me goosebumps. My thin Care Bears nightgown with ruffles along the bottom did nothing to keep me warm. Because of the fluorescent lights pouring in from the kitchen into the dining room, shadows rose from the dining chairs and shelves in frightening and angular ways.

I ran through the dining room and swung open the wooden saloon doors to the kitchen, which slapped the kitchen counters before swinging closed again behind me. Aunt Stephanie, Jim's sister, was sitting straight across the kitchen from me, in the breakfast nook, with a ragged towel around her shoulders. A box in the middle of the kitchen separated us like a waist-high barricade. Mom stood behind her, and her Native American skin looked even darker in comparison to my aunt's pale face. The smoke from the cigarette pressed between my mom's lips forced her right eye to blink as she wrapped each curl.

I remember my aunt's face: her smile and the fluffy cotton coils that separated her rows of curls and protected her scalp from the chemicals. I remember the sound of tissue crinkling as Mom wrapped the hair around paper and blue curlers.

Suddenly, my aunt's eyes went wide, and her mouth twisted into a shout. I didn't pay attention to what she said. Instead, I slid toward her like a baseball player skidding to home base. But the stupid big box was in my way.

I slapped my hands on top of it with a *thwap* and immediately knew something was wrong. Burning, blistering pain shot through my body. I tried to scream but it got stuck in my throat. Tears streamed down my face, and an inferno raged beneath the skin on my fingers.

The box was the bubbling kerosene heater.

I yanked my hands back from the scorching metal, and red, seared flesh replaced the white pudge on my fingers and palms. In an instant, Mom stamped out her cigarette. She hollered for Jim, who must've been working on his bike outside in the garage. He ran in wearing an old greasy shirt and pair of jeans, just as Mom stuffed my hands into a bowl filled with ice, replacing the heat with the sting of regret. It was the same green Tupperware bowl we used for Jell-O.

I don't remember what happened to my aunt's perm. Those chemicals can't stay there, so someone must've rinsed them out, but the commotion swallowed me up and I couldn't focus on anything but my burns.

In the car a moment later, flashes of red flew by my window from the stoplights we zipped through on the way to the hospital. Jim drove faster than usual, and my head bobbed around like a little toy. Before we made it across town, the ice melted. Each bump deepened the pain.

The parking lot at the hospital was empty except for a straggle of cars sitting beneath buzzing streetlamps. We got a good spot, close to the entrance. Jim carried me, and Mom carried my bowl. Their shoes plodded across the cracked gravel and into the icy hospital. I wished I had a blanket.

In the corner of the empty waiting room sat a tube television. I think a sitcom was playing, or maybe a game show. I didn't watch, but I heard the voices, the laughter, and the clapping. The scent of rubbing alcohol filled my nose. *Yuck.* It made my stomach do flips.

I sat in a gray chair made of hard plastic and thin fabric and waited for someone to call my name. Silently, I promised myself I'd never forget what fire can do.

"Danielle?" a nurse in blue scrubs called from the door.

"It's okay, Pumpkin. We'll get you fixed up," said Mom.

On Camping

It started with my parents nestling me between boxes of food in the enclosed bed of Jim's white pickup. Jim and my mother softened the metal frame with old quilts and a pillow from home, and I rode in that spot from downtown Toledo to Camp Pokagon in Indiana, an hour and a half away.

"It'll be an adventure," said Jim as he scratched his orange mustache and smiled. He tucked his cigarettes into his flannel shirt and shut the back of the truck. As we set off, each bump in the road made the supplies rattle and truck bed bounce. It was closer to a near-death, holy Jesus experience than an adventure.

It wasn't the least bit safe, but it was the eighties. This was during a time when you could smoke on a plane, so riding in a truck bed with the possibility of blunt objects flying and impaling you seemed perfectly okay.

At Pokagon, the adults set up camp at a gravel opening near the tree line. We stayed in a blue tent that resembled the ripped tarp Jim used to cover his speedboat. I couldn't tell the difference. The air inside the tent stuck to my skin with humidity and mustiness, and there was this strange smell. Maybe mold? Each time I crawled inside, I pinched my nose and held my breath.

The mud at the campsite stuck to the bottom of my sneakers like goopy quicksand sucking me down. But I didn't want to complain, because if I did, then Jim would call me names like *whiner* and *wuss*. Mom said he liked to joke with me, but I didn't find him funny.

Instead, I found a place to play with my dolls on the picnic table and pretended to have fun, until Barbie's boyfriend, Ken, got a splinter in his foot and Mom had to pull it out with tweezers.

When bugs flew too close, I swatted and flicked them.

I had two choices for going pee: the woods with a roll of toilet paper, or hike for what seemed like a mile to the bathroom. I wouldn't be caught dead outside with my jean shorts around my ankles, so each time I had to use the restroom I made Mom hike with me. And trust me, the bathroom wasn't much better than the woods. Bugs zipped around and landed on my bare knees, and the light above my head flickered and buzzed while I tried to wipe. The whole building smelled like pee, so I had to plug my nose.

That first night, Jim built a fire. The heat radiating from the orange and blue flames warmed and dried out my dewy cheeks, but I kept my distance because I was afraid to get hurt by fire again. Once the flames were so hot my eyeballs burned, we roasted puffy white marshmallows until they blackened on the outside and turned gooey in the middle. I pulled mine off the stick and shoved the whole thing in my mouth. My fingers were a sticky mess, so I sucked on them.

After Mom dumped sand on the embers, we trudged to our tent for the night.

"Goodnight," she said as she turned off the battery-operated lantern.

"Night," I said, burrowing my head deep inside my Barbie sleeping bag to muffle the sound of the crickets.

My eyes were heavy, but the lumpy ground made it hard to fall asleep. Eventually I drifted off, but right away something outside the tent woke me. I heard the crinkle of a plastic bag as an animal or *something* rummaged through the garbage. I thought for sure it was a bear who would eat us all for a midnight snack.

"Dad! Something's outside the tent!" I whispered to wake up Jim. I poked him in his beer belly.

"What do you want, Danielle?" he grumbled and swatted at me. "I was sleeping."

"Something's out there." I pointed to the tent wall.

He unzipped the side of the tent, and cool air sifted in, mixing with the mustiness. His head poked outside, and I pulled my hot pink blanket up to my chin and closed my eyes.

If it had been a bear, Jim would have been dead.

"It's a raccoon diggin' through the garbage." Jim snorted. He turned to rummage through a duffel bag until he found his 45mm and snapped a picture.

The next morning, Mom stayed back at the campsite to drink her coffee in peace while Jim and I went to check out an old toboggan run. Age and weather had splintered the outdoor wooden steps, and it was a steep climb. But what else was there to do? I was sick of the muddy, smelly campsite. Halfway up, I climbed onto Jim's back because my legs were small and tired. I couldn't keep up with him anymore.

At the top of the steps, Jim said, "Oh shit," so I peered over his shoulder. A nest bigger than a watermelon, swarming with hornets, hung inside the toboggan shed. Jim turned to run back down the steps with me still clinging to his shoulders, but the pissed hornets chased us, swarming, zipping, and stinging.

Jim kept running, never wincing once.

The hornets got me in the ankle and behind my knee. Two times. Maybe more. The stings quickly went from warm to fiery, and soon both my legs itched. I wanted to scratch them, but Jim warned me not to. I listened.

Back at camp, Mom rubbed something that looked like a Chapstick on the stings, then sent me to lie down in the tent. I had never been happier to see the blue tarp, feel the humidity sticking to my cheeks, and smell the mold.

My first childhood camping trip was also my last.

Red Flashing Lights

Mom sat in the driver's seat of our gray Chevy Celebrity after she buckled me in the backseat. The corduroy seats itched the back of my knees, so I kept tugging on my fluffy pink skirt hem. I played with the window crank on the door, turning it back and forth. Each time the window opened, warm air seeped in and stuck inside my nose. I kicked my feet back and forth, trying to touch my toes against the carpet, but at five years old, my legs were too short to reach.

Mom and I car-danced to Madonna's "Papa Don't Preach." It was like any other day riding home from school until she gasped and slammed on her brakes. Our heads flew forward then flung back against the seats with a *thud*. I stopped kicking and car-dancing. Stopped playing with the window. Stopped breathing for the shortest moment.

"Oh, God!" Mom shuddered. I exhaled, and the world rotated again. "That car hit the little girl so hard she…" Her voice trailed off as she raked her hands through her long hair, tying it back at her neck. The car clicked into park and her seatbelt raveled up, all in the same second.

Everything stood still as we connected glances in the rear-view mirror. There, in her big brown eyes, I saw concern and love, then determination and strength. All before she blinked.

She climbed out of her seat, shut her door with a *bang*, and stopped in front of my window. "You stay here," she commanded. Bravery filled each line on her face in a way that I had never seen.

I gulped down a breath bubble and scratched the corduroy seat to feel the fibers under my nails. I nodded.

"I mean it, Danielle," she said.

"Okay, Mommy."

She was already jogging away. I didn't know what had happened, only that Mom left me alone in the car. It scared me and made my heart race.

I craned my head to peek out the window, and the smell of gasoline fumes and burned rubber overwhelmed me. The busy street was near home, but I couldn't tell which one it was. I saw a girl lying face-down on the pavement with French fries and broken glass scattered around her. She wasn't much bigger than me. And behind the girl was a car parked at an awkward angle. Its windshield was caved in, its spiderweb of glass refracting bits of light. I turned away from the scene, the blood, and the bits of Happy Meal scattered on the ground. Mom rushed to the center of the crowd that had gathered and knelt down to the girl.

I avoided the scene out of my window for what seemed like hours. Sirens and voices carried in from just beyond our car. Red flashing lights shined through the window, but I didn't once lift my head. I cowered in my seat, humming the Madonna song that was no longer playing.

Eventually, everything slowed. People hushed. Lights and sirens faded. Traffic resumed.

My mom opened her door, sat in the driver's seat, cradled her head in her hands, and wept.

She said, "I tried, Danielle, but I couldn't save her life."

Keep Pedaling

Jim cleared the cars from the driveway and opened the gate to give me plenty of space to ride. With Mom's Hosta plants to my right and Jim's railroad ties framing the driveway to the left, I perched myself on the banana seat. I inhaled the smell of Cheerios cooking down the road at the General Mills plant and glared down the empty driveway, gripping the bubblegum pink handlebars of my new bike. It was the bike I had to have: pink and white with tassels and a basket, complete with a silver bell on the right handlebar.

"I won't let go. Promise," Jim said. I was only six, but I knew the shtick. If he didn't let go, I'd never learn to ride a bike on my own.

I put both feet on the pedals. Jim put one hand on the bar behind the seat and one on the middle of the handlebars. I felt unsteady without training wheels, but Jim kept the bike balanced.

"Ready?" he asked. I could smell the coffee on his breath. *Yuck.* I gritted my teeth and clutched the handlebars harder.

"Ready."

He pushed, and I pedaled. At first, he kept his promise and didn't let go. We cruised from the back of the driveway to the other end by the street so I could get an understanding of the way my bike needed balancing. He ran along beside me.

"Good," he said. "Keep pedaling."

I don't know where Don was at the time. Maybe he was with another woman, teaching another kid to ride a bike. I didn't think he loved me, otherwise he would have tried to be there for important stuff.

I didn't think Jim loved me either. I thought I was a formality, part of the package that came with my mother. I figured Jim could take me or leave me, and it wouldn't matter to him.

Still, there he was.

I pedaled faster, toward the open garage door and the boat inside it that Jim was fixing for a friend. Without warning, he let go.

"Pedal!" he hollered. I tried, but I lost my focus and the bike wobbled then tipped to the right. I tramped my foot on the pavement.

"Darn," I said. This happened several more times, back and forth on the driveway. Each time it ended the same. Jim let go, and I tipped over.

"You'll figure it out," he said. Jim walked toward me while lighting a cigarette. He blew the smoke out of his nose while he scratched the cleft on his chin. His chocolate eyes stared into the distance. I wished I looked like him and maybe had his last name, so I wouldn't feel like such an outsider in my family. I didn't want to look like Don and share a last name with him anymore.

I played with the tassels while Jim took a break and smoked his cigarette down to the butt. When he finished, he flicked it into the gravel beside the driveway. I was ready to give up and go inside to watch *Jem and the Holograms*, when Jim belched and said, "Let's try something different."

He raked his hands through his feathered brown hair and shuffled to the end of the driveway. I followed, guiding my bike along with me. We set up the same way: feet on pedals, hands on handlebars, and Jim holding the bike upright. But this time we aimed my bike down the sidewalk—rectangle patches of concrete that stretched on for what seemed like forever.

"Remember: pedal hard. I got you," he said.

I nodded, pressing my lips into a tight line and focusing on the spot where the sidewalk disappeared and met the horizon.

Before I knew it, Jim let go, and I was still upright, pedaling away.

She Sees Seashells[1]

"**G**o to your room. NOW!" Mom shouted. I had just talked back to her, an out-of-character act for me. But I was six, and I'd recently been uprooted from my childhood home so Mom could care for Grandpa, who had a brand-new green oxygen tank. His sickness scared me.

So many things changed that year. I saw my real father less than ever. Not that I'd seen him much before that anyway; he was more like a shadow than a real person to me. Mom said Jim was officially going to be my stepdad. They were planning a wedding at the courthouse because Mom had a baby in her belly. She said it would be my new sister or brother, but I didn't want another kid to share my stuff with.

On days when Grandpa was doing well, Mom and I would move the coffee table to dance in circles around the living room to disco music. That day, Grandpa wasn't doing well, which meant Mom wasn't doing well either. She had a shorter temper, cried a lot, and only played sad stuff on her record player.

I sulked to my temporary bedroom, a tiny space with four annoying yellow walls, and I shut the door. My real bedroom sat on the other side of the city. Mom couldn't work while she cared for Grandpa, so Jim had rented out our house to keep the bank from taking it. I missed our home.

Only my Barbies, shoved under my bed, were brought for me to play with. Most of my things had to stay back in my toybox; not enough room here. I had grown to hate the dolls and all their perfect smiles. So I sat on my bed and cried for Mom to relieve me of my sentence.

"I'm sorry, Mommy! Can I come out yet?" I asked. No answer.

I stared at the framed bedtime prayer that hung next to the door,

---

1 Versions of this essay have been published on *Dead Housekeeping* and *The Mindful Word*.

wishing my mom would come and release me. Then my eyes drifted to the high shelf on my wall, and I caught sight of them: Mom's seashells. A hundred or so small ones were piled in mason jars, while the big ones sat directly on the shelf: conch shells, sand dollars, and starfish, each one fragile and unique.

Mom had collected them years ago on a vacation in Florida, long before she and Don had me, back when she was skinny and tan and wore things like terry-cloth jumpsuits. When we moved into the apartment above Grandpa's, Mom had nowhere to display her collection, so Jim mounted a shelf in my room. Although I had already shared my space with the shells for months, it had never occurred to me to climb up and get them. For as long as I remembered, even on Custer, they had always just been a display. On occasion, Mom would bring them down for me, to shake the sand dollars or listen to the ocean in the conch shells. She'd tell me stories about Florida, and how sunny and warm it was there. It was her favorite place. But the shells never stayed down for long. She always put them away just as quickly as she let me hold them. They were special to her, from a time before me, when life was easier. The shells always made her smile.

I thought maybe if I got them down for her, she would be less sad.

I climbed down from my bed and pulled out the bottom drawer of my dresser to use as a ladder. I stepped onto my pajamas, perfectly folded inside the drawer, and the dresser wobbled. I paused for a moment and considered whether I should go on, then decided it was fine. I pushed the three plaster figurines Mom painted to look like me aside and wrapped my fingers around the top of the dresser, at the back. Then I hiked my legs up onto the top one at a time, crouching all four limbs on the surface. Suddenly I thought that climbing onto the dresser wasn't the best idea. The top wasn't so high from the ground, but the thought of standing up on it turned the room around me like my Sit 'n Spin.

I hunkered there, just beneath the shelf, determined to get the big conch shell so Mom and I could listen to the ocean. I didn't want to think about Grandpa's tubes that snaked from his nose to the oxygen tank anymore, and I was sure Mom didn't either.

Inch by inch I stood, careful to keep the dresser steady. I stayed quiet because I wanted to surprise her. Plus, Mom would get mad if she knew I was climbing; she would have wanted me to ask to hold the shells. I stood and had just stretched my hand up, inches away from the conch shell, when the door swung open.

"Danielle, you all right?" Mom asked from my bedroom threshold. She startled me and my arms swung up in a windmill motion, first one then the other. My right hand bumped the shelf, which wasn't secured to the wall like it should have been.

It toppled sideways and sent seashells crashing to the floor, leaving me standing there on the dresser, surrounded by a mess.

"My seashells!" Mom shouted. She stood at the door, clutching the frame. "What were you thinking?" She let go of the wall, hands trembling as she wiped moisture from her eyes with her fingertips. "I can never get those back. They were special, Danielle." All her shells lay on the floor, some in pieces, some only chipped. Her head hung when she bent to pick up a few of the bigger ones that could be salvaged. She placed them on my dresser.

"I thought they would make you happy," I said as new tears welled up in my eyes.

Her expression softened. "You could've gotten hurt."

"Sorry, Mommy."

She picked me up and put me on the bed. "Stay there. I'll get the broom."

When she left, I leaned over the edge of my bed. The biggest conch shell was within reach and still in one piece. I picked it up, held it close to my ear and listened to the *whoosh*. I closed my eyes and imagined the ocean Mom had told me about. I had never been to the beach, but I knew it was better than the yellow room on Lagrange Street.

She walked into the bedroom with the broom and dustpan, and I held the shell up to ask, "Wanna listen?"

No Place Like Home

Before my grandpa's stroke, I would sit on his round belly and ask him if the bump above his heart hurt. I'd lightly press my fingers against the square shape protruding from his chest, and Grandpa would smile wide to show his toothless gums.

"Naw, baby girl. That's my ticker," he'd say.

I imagined a tiny clock ticking away inside his chest, like the Tin Man.

His second stroke hit him like a tornado, turning everything upside down. He couldn't move one side of his body, so Jim moved Grandpa's bed into the living room. There were times I wanted to climb back on his belly, but I didn't. I was too scared. I thought I would catch whatever he had.

Mom didn't let me play outside much because she thought I'd get run over by a speeding car. Even though Lagrange Street had been her home as a child, she had grown up and moved on, away from the poorest part of town. It bothered her to move back.

Our bright apartment was narrow and open, leading from the living room to the dining room and finally the kitchen. It looked identical to my grandparents' house downstairs, except instead of maroon carpet, we had old oak floors and linoleum.

"Wanna listen to the cop scanner, baby girl?" Grandma asked one Saturday while Mom cleaned upstairs.

"Yeah!" I squealed and sat on Grandma's blue velvet ottoman, and we listened to the calls. Most of it sounded garbled and full of static. I liked how the people who talked in number code sounded rushed and full of coffee. It was more entertaining than *The Wizard of Oz*.

Before dinner one evening, Mom burned her hand on the antique cast-iron stove.

"Ah, Christ!" she yelled.

"What happened?" I hollered, running in from the living room where I had built a two-level house for my Barbies from the coffee table to the floor. I made beds out of bathroom washcloths because we had no money for the doll mansion I wanted, the one with three floors and an elevator operated by string.

"I burned my hand on this piece-of-shit stove. Don't get too close to it." Mom had her hand under the running faucet. Her palm turned slightly pink from the burn. It reminded me of the kerosene heater years ago.

"Can I help?" I asked, slinking farther from the stove.

"I'll be all right. But maybe you should go play with Jude. I'll watch you walk next door." Mom wrapped a couple ice cubes in a ragged dish towel and nudged me toward the front door.

"Okay," I muttered.

I liked Jude. He liked wrestling as much as me, only he called it "wrassling." Jude was a pudgy boy with shaggy brown hair who lived with his grandpa and grandma in the house next door. At his house, we played with Jake the Snake and Hulk Hogan dolls, then took turns pulling on Stretch Armstrong.

Their house smelled like pipe tobacco and fatty meat because his grandma was always frying up something in the kitchen. She had big brown hair, round coke bottle glasses, and a soft, round body to match. His grandpa rarely got up from the dining room table, where he played cards and smoked his pipe all day long.

When Jude wasn't home, and I wanted to get away from everyone in my family, I would sit on the steps in the hallway that connected the two houses. I'd stare at the cracks and chips in the yellow walls, imagining they were part of a roadmap to someplace over the rainbow where Grandpa was all better.

Grandpa's ticker stopped that spring in second grade. It happened while I was away at school. Like the Tin Man, he followed that yellow brick road home.

Oh, Sister

"When do I get my bubblegum cigar?" I asked Jim. I was promised I would get one when my little sister was born, and because I was in second grade, that was about as much as I cared about her in the beginning. My nose was pressed to the glass of the window in the newborn unit, and my breath made small circles of steam underneath. I turned back to face Jim, who was sitting in a chair against the wall.

He yawned and combed his hands through his disheveled hair. "Danielle, don't be rude. You'll get it eventually." He closed his eyes for a long moment.

"I want to go home." I sulked, stepping away from the glass and shuffling my weight to my left hip. "Hospitals are boring, and they smell funny."

Earlier that year, Jim had married Mom at the courthouse when Brittany was still in Mom's belly. I got to wear a pretty pink dress with puffy sleeves, white gloves, and my little wicker Easter hat; Mom even gave me my very own bouquet. But I was still sour because I had to miss *Jem and the Holograms*. Instead of watching my favorite show, we stood in a small office with ratty blue office carpet and big windows that overlooked the Maumee River. The room smelled like mothballs, and it was so hot that my nose burned and eyes watered. That's where Jim and Mom said, "I do."

When Brittany and Mom came home to Lagrange Street, Mom put her crib in the dining room—there were no bedrooms left. The doctors sent machines from the hospital, because they thought there was something wrong with Brittany's heart. Mom went from coloring in my Lisa Frank coloring book and dressing Barbies with me to changing dirty diapers, feeding Brittany, and listening to those monitors beep. As much as

I wanted to blame my sister for flipping my life sideways, I couldn't. She was this little ball of squishy skin with big brown eyes and a cute grin. All I wanted to do was protect her.

After what seemed like a few months, the hospital collected their machines. Brittany's heart ended up being fine, thank goodness. Our family didn't need any more sadness. Mom and Jim must've felt the same way, because for Christmas that year, I finally got the doll mansion with an elevator.

Presence: Part I

The day I turned eight in 1989, Don knocked on the door at Mom's house.

"I came to say happy birthday," he said when I opened it.

I thanked him through the screen door.

"Hard to believe you're already eight." He looked away, so I followed his gaze toward his beater car in the driveway, still running.

I poked my finger through a hole in the screen the size of a nickel. It had started with a tiny slit I jabbed my pinky into, and over the years—with the Jehovah's Witnesses, neighbors selling Girl Scout cookies, and Don occasionally stopping by—the hole had gotten bigger.

He wore a faded jean jacket and a trucker cap. His pale skin looked ashen through the screen that separated us.

"I brought your present." He pulled a cassette from his pocket and waved it at me. That year, Mom had bought me a Walkman to listen to all my cassettes. She and Jim couldn't afford much else other than that.

I stepped outside the door onto our cement front porch. Green plants with brown tips sprawled from the planters. Soon, they'd die off and sleep for the winter. "Thanks."

"Is it the right album?" he asked. At that point, our relationship consisted of nothing more than the occasional gift or card. He offered no advice or scolding. He never called to ask what television shows I liked, what food I hated, or the names of my best friends. He didn't know me well enough to know what I wanted, so I had told him over the phone the week prior.

I looked at the front. The New Kids on the Block band members sat in a sleigh with jolly grins on their faces. "Yeah. It's the only one I don't have." I looked back to Don. "Will I see you again?"

"I hope so. But not for a while. I've been driving trucks down south."

"Can I come visit you in Tennessee?" I wanted to love him as much as any child loved her father. But I was cautious. I didn't get too close, because I didn't want to get hurt by him again. I craned my neck up to see him. Long dark hair, same color as mine, fell almost to his shoulders. Yes, I looked like him, but I didn't know him. I only knew that he liked race cars and drove a semi-truck.

"Sure. Listen, I've got to get going now." He scratched his cheek and adjusted his cap.

"Okay. Well, thanks, Dad. Love you."

"See ya, kid." He waved and walked away.

Satin Things on Christmas

The ham had nearly finished cooking in the oven. The smell of white birch burning and popping in the fireplace filled the air. Beer flowed from Grandpa's keg and filled every adult's cup. My aunt had just told a story about some client at the firm, and everyone broke into laughter. I didn't get the joke. It was the Christmas of 1991, and I was ten.

Brittany, three at the time, and some of my younger cousins were busy building with Grandma's set of Lincoln Logs. I could have joined in with them, but they would only topple my house and ruin all my hard work. So instead I sat on the floor leaning against Mom's thigh, next to Jim's feet.

Grandma's eight cats took turns rubbing up against me while purring. I didn't really like cats. Still don't. But they were Grandma's cats, so I let them do their thing. Occasionally I'd rub one between the eyes or behind the ears, but mostly I ignored them.

"Alright. Time for presents!" Grandma exclaimed. She sat at the front by the tree and handed out the gifts with a wide grin on her face. Her gray hair was curled close to her head thanks to a recent perm from Mom. "This one's for you, Danielle!" She winked, then handed me a box wrapped in shiny green paper with a big red satin bow taped to the top.

I thought for sure it was gloves. That's what she gave me every year: the little cotton ones that come in a two-pack: pink and gray, or black and red.

Once, she got me stilts. That year was special, I guess. I loved those stilts. It took all summer to learn to walk on them without tipping forward, and by the time I was nine I could run on them if I had too.

The box was too small for something cool like stilts.

I pulled off the red bow, ripped the shiny wrapping paper, and used my index fingernail to slice through the tape sealing up the cardboard. I opened the top of the box, pulled the white tissue paper away, and gulped.

As soon as my eyes caught a glance of the thin, satiny triangles, I slammed the lid shut.

"What'd you get?" Mom asked. She tilted her head back to see through the bottom half of her bifocals.

"Nothing." My cheeks burned, but not from the fire crackling beside me.

"Don't be rude, Danielle. Show us what you got," Mom insisted, raising her eyebrows.

Everyone around me stopped to watch. They opened no presents, sipped no drinks. The room filled with silence; no laughter or cats meowing. It was me and my present, front and center.

"Open it up," Jim said, kicking my hip.

I pulled the box close. "Do I have to?" I whined. Mom nodded.

I opened the box and pulled out the white 30 AA bra by the straps and turned away, my face blushing.

"It's a trainer! Your first bra, Danielle," Grandma gushed.

"Thanks, Grandma." I stuffed the thin fabric and elastic back in the box. "I really love it."

"How sweet!" exclaimed Mom. Aunts and uncles returned to their drinks and conversation.

"You don't have much, but you can practice wearing one," Grandma continued. "It's got some padding, too." I heard my older cousins stifling snickers and snorts.

Unlike my bra, I was too big to hide in a box.

Lulu's Pond

"See you later, Danielle!"

Stacy, my neighbor from two doors down, waved before she climbed into her mom's minivan. It was the beginning of July, the summer after my fourth-grade year. She had a pillow clutched under her arm and headphones already on her head; her family was heading to Myrtle Beach.

"Have fun! I'll miss you!" I shouted. It was Sunday, and they would be gone for two full weeks.

I had played with Stacy and her brother every day that summer. We swam in their pool and rode bikes to the park. We flagged down the ice cream truck and sat on my cement porch eating orange push-ups with Fred Flintstone on the wrapper.

I couldn't survive two weeks without my friends. I'd die from loneliness.

I reluctantly waved back as she settled into her bucket seat.

Inside the house, I bawled. "My friends left, Mom!" Because she was short, I was already up to her shoulders. I knew one day I'd be taller than her. But for now, I leaned my head against her and smelled her patchouli perfume.

"We can't afford a vacation to the ocean," she said. She leaned her head on my head, but never looked up from the dishes she was scrubbing.

I pulled away. "That's not fair! I hate being poor." I stomped up to my room and slammed the door. I stayed there, half-sulking and half-singing to the radio until I heard a knock at the door.

"Yeah?" I asked.

"Can I come in?"

"Sure," I sighed, flopping my head against my pillow.

Mom opened the door and sat at the foot of the bed. "I'm sorry we don't have money to do things like go to the ocean," she said, almost in a whisper. Her head dipped.

"I know." I gazed out the window at the locust tree. I called it the cigar tree because of the long brown seed pods it dropped. When the wind blew, the seeds rattled inside their "cigars" and made a sound similar to that of shaking a beaded necklace or maraca.

"Do you want to go to the beach this Saturday?" she asked, perking up.

"Duh!" I shouted, turning my focus back to her.

"Not the ocean. The beach," she repeated.

"Okay. Whatever. Yeah, I want to go to the beach."

I was certain Saturday would never come. Every day dragged on as I sat in our unfinished plywood living room on an oversized armchair reading R.L. Stine books, while Brittany played on the rug beside me and Mom put laundry in the machines tucked behind folding doors in the corner. Throughout my childhood, Mom was always washing, drying, and folding. The scent of clean clothes made her happy, especially since Jim had bought a used dryer off his buddy, and Mom didn't have to hang the clothes outside to dry anymore. She must've washed seven loads in the days leading up to Saturday, and I finished three books.

But finally, Saturday arrived.

Mom loaded our bright plastic sand toys, worn-in beach towels, and folding beach chairs into the minivan. She packed a cooler full of Capri Suns and sandwiches of Jif smeared on Wonder Bread. Jim stayed behind to work on the living room addition he was finishing on the back of the house.

We drove to Lulu's Pond at Totem Pole Park, a campground in the middle of Michigan. Three large totem poles towered over our minivan at the entrance of the dirt road leading up to the beach.

"Mom? Where are we?" I asked, peering out the window.

"The beach."

"This place isn't a beach." I shook my head.

"It is. You'll see."

We parked the car in a gravel lot, loaded Brittany and our stuff into the wagon, and walked down a short dirt path to Lulu's. No matter where I stood at the pond's edge, I could see across to the other side, a brown pool sloshing in the center of a wooded area. It didn't smell like the ocean or a lake because it wasn't. It smelled like wet earth and spruce trees.

Lulu's didn't have a beach with sand grains we could sift through our fingers. The "sand" was actually mud, and it stuck to the bottom of my flip-flops, shoving them farther onto my feet. I ran barefoot and let the mud squish between my toes. Water-logged sticks floated near the pond's edge where we played. The water didn't lap at my ankles or make roaring waves. It was still, except for the occasional ripple from someone jumping in.

Twenty-something big-haired ladies in bikinis lay on rubber tri-fold beach chairs surrounding the "beach" side of the pond. Some kids, mostly teenage boys, splashed into the center of the pond from a raft.

Mom laid out the chairs and towels on the driest spot she could find and dialed our battery-operated boombox to the oldies station. Then she slathered on coconut tanning oil and sipped pops under the sun while Brittany built mud castles. Every couple of minutes, my eyes flickered toward the boys swimming in the deep end. The boys smiled and winked, inviting me in, but I didn't go because of the slimy, scaly fish that might nibble at my ankles. Plus, murky water made me think of the movie *Friday the Thirteenth*. I was contemplating which was worse when Mom interrupted my thoughts.

"Who's your best friend?" she asked.

"Probably Stacy." I shrugged, pushing my steamy sunglasses to the top of my sweaty nose. Stacy had become my best friend mostly because of her proximity to our house. Stacy was fourteen months younger than me, and during the school year we each had our own friends, but during the summers our friendship flowered. I'd often find her knocking on my door to play while I was still shoveling Fruity Pebbles into my mouth, watching *Saved by the Bell*.

"I like Stacy. She's a good kid. Think any of those boys are cute?" Mom pulled her dollar store sunglasses down from her eyes, and I noticed how perfectly plucked her eyebrows were. The older I got, the bushier my eyebrows seemed to get, and I wondered when she'd teach me to thin them.

"Maybe the one in red, I guess." His thin, muscular body and blond hair reminded me of Zac Morris from Bayside High. The thought of holding his hand made my stomach feel strange.

"Why don't you go talk to him?" she said, tilting her head to the side and shifting closer to me in her chair.

"Mom! Seriously, I don't want to talk about boys anymore. Can we change the subject?" I pulled my knees into my chest and turned away from her gaze, blushing. I didn't mind that she was trying to figure me out: an elementary school kid, *almost* junior high teen. And I wasn't afraid to be seen with her. Not yet, anyway. I liked being by her, watching her, and mimicking her beauty. But I didn't want to talk about boys with her. That was just weird.

When Brittany started fussing and the sun began its descent behind the trees, we packed up our stuff and climbed into the van, which was an oven from sitting in the sun all day. I seared my leg on the seatbelt buckle. "Ouch!"

"What happened?" Mom asked as she heaved the wagon into the trunk.

"I burned my thigh, but I'm okay." I rubbed the red spot on my skin.

Mom liked the windows down, so we rode for thirty minutes with our hair snapping in the stifling wind. The back of my dirt-caked legs stuck to the seat with sweat. Still, a smile of sweet satisfaction was stuck on my face. Being outside, away from home, near water with Mom and Brittany was nice—it wasn't the ocean, and it wasn't far away, but it was still a vacation.

A week later, Stacy came back home with souvenir necklaces made of shells, a neon pink t-shirt, and beads sewn into her hair. She handed me a friendship bracelet with my name stitched onto it and asked if I'd like to come swimming in her pool.

"Heck yes," I said. While we swam, I told her about my new crush— Zac Morris from the pond.

"That sounds so fun," she said, pursing her lips. "It takes so long to get to Myrtle Beach. I wish my family went someplace like Lulu's too."

Turns out we both had decent vacations that year.

Night Ride

Brittany and I played all day in the plastic baby pool Mom and Jim had set up on the driveway. We had colorful cups, a blow-up ring, and six inches of water to splash in. It doesn't take much to make kids happy.

While we played, Jim worked on his money-pit motorcycle and listened to Aerosmith on his garage stereo, humming along. No matter how little we had, Jim always kept his bike running. Sometimes I hated how he seemed to love the bike more than us.

Mom hung laundry to dry on the line, chain-smoking cigarettes. The dryer had broken again, and there wasn't money for a new one. Laundry never smelled clean after hanging on the line to dry. Instead, it stiffened and stunk like dirt.

In the house, unpaid bills cluttered the counter. Mom pushed them out of the way to open and warm a can of beef stew. When it bubbled in the pot, she poured it over cooked white rice. They couldn't afford much fresh food, but they kept us fed. We ate in the kitchen, on the couch, wherever we could, because car parts covered the dining room table, collecting dust.

Mom fed Brittany baby food she had bought with money borrowed from my Velcro wallet, then tucked her into her crib beneath the warm, soft glow of her bedside lamp.

"Wanna go for a motorcycle ride?" Jim asked me later that night, while he strummed on his guitar.

I shrugged. "Sure."

"Go get your shoes."

I hustled my feet into white canvas Kmart sneakers and ran outside. The sun had slid below the horizon, streetlights had buzzed to life, and birds had gone to bed. I took a deep breath and smelled Trix cereal cooking at the General Mills plant two blocks away. There wasn't a breeze, so the heat from the day clung to my neck like a wool scarf.

"Be careful, Jim!" Mom called as the wooden screen door slammed shut. The spring that was supposed to help it close slowly had snapped ages ago. Over time, we got used to the creaking, rattling, and the sound of wood slapping wood.

Jim rolled his eyes and flicked his half-smoked cigarette into the street. "I'm always careful," he mumbled. He turned to me. "Wear this." He handed me his helmet, then put on a pair of clear sunglasses to shield his eyes from bugs. No helmet for him. There weren't any helmet laws back then, so either he trusted his luck to protect his brains from the pavement, or he couldn't afford a second helmet. Maybe both.

I put the adult-sized helmet on. Though he tightened the chinstrap as much as he could, it continued to wobble each time I turned my head. After the helmet was as secure as it could be, he helped me climb onto the back of his bike.

"Don't let your leg touch the exhaust," Jim warned. My feet dangled inches from the chrome pipes.

"Why?" I asked.

"It'll burn like hell, and your ma won't be happy." I looked wide-eyed at the exhaust and adjusted my leg accordingly, wedging my feet into the safe spot he pointed to.

He climbed on and kicked the starter. The engine sputtered and roared to life.

"Hold on," he said. "But not around my neck. You'll choke me."

I wrapped my arms around his belly and grabbed fistfuls of his holey sweatshirt. With my head so close to his back, I smelled car grease and stale smoke, but also home. Jim walked the bike backward down the driveway until he reached the street, then rolled the throttle before we disappeared into the night.

We took winding back roads from Toledo, Ohio, to Luna Pier, Michigan. We passed the mall, then nothing but flat, open fields of corn. There were no streetlights or stoplights, only his bike's single headlight illuminating the gravel in front of us. The growl of the engine filled the silence between us. We couldn't have talked if we wanted to, but I didn't want to. I needed the distance from home to try and forget about how little we had.

When we pulled onto the pier, Jim brought the bike to a gradual stop. Stillness and the smell of lake water replaced the vibration of the engine. He helped me off the bike, and we meandered along a cement sidewalk to a park bench to watch the moonlight reflect off the ripples in the water. Without as much light pollution from the city, the stars shone brighter out there. I thought the darkness would swallow me up in one big gulp. It was hard to tell if the water was reflecting the sky, or maybe the other way around. Nothing was wrong out on that pier: no unpaid bills cluttering the counter or car parts littering the dining room table. Time stopped. My family's problems seemed so small and insignificant as I looked out into the great big sky.

"Is this why you like your bike so much?" I asked.

"Sure is." He lit a cigarette.

Even without the noise of the road, we didn't say much; we listened and watched and smelled.

Eventually, Jim said, "Ready to go?"

"I guess," I said.

But the ride home wasn't worth remembering.

Geauga Lake

Geauga Lake in Aurora, Ohio, was the epitome of American excess when it was open: part waterpark with bright blue water slides and a massive wave pool; part theme park with twisting, dropping rides. No matter a child's fancy, she could find it in Aurora.

Except for me.

"I don't wanna go to Geauga Lake!" I wailed as we packed into the minivan. "I wanna see Shamu!" SeaWorld sat on the opposite side of Geauga Lake. So close, but still so far. I folded my arms across my chest and pouted. Sometimes if I turned my chin to just the right position, Mom would cave.

"We go to SeaWorld every year," she said. "You'll have fun at Geauga Lake too. Just give it a chance. Besides, family vacations aren't supposed to be all about fun. It's more about spending time together."

Uncle Matt and Aunt Beatrice followed us in their minivan. Uncle Matt was a quiet man who wore a pocket protector in his short-sleeved button-down, even on Saturdays. Aunt Beatrice, well ... she talked enough for the both of them. They had their kids in their van, too: Trina, their youngest, was the same age as me; and my cousin Stan, who was old enough to be my uncle and had hair longer than mine. I loved them, but to me it didn't matter because I also hated water parks.

My shoulders slumped back into the seat. "The only reason we're even going is because Aunt Beatrice is making us."

"That's not true. And you'll have fun with Trina. She's your favorite cousin."

I frowned the whole way to Aurora, but it was futile.

When we arrived, I slathered on the strongest SPF Mom had in her wicker beach bag. Somehow I'd ended up with my father's Scottish skin instead of the Native American glow my mom, sister, aunt, and cousins were blessed with. My fair and freckled body burned to a crisp without protection.

Over the morning, we rode carnival-like rides, the spinning ones that never get too far off the ground. I liked those, so things were fun for me until I got nauseous on the big swaying boat after eating too much cotton candy.

"Can we do something else?" I asked.

"Sure," said Uncle Matt.

We worked our way toward the water slides. I stared up at them from the safety of the concrete sidewalk. All their twists, turns, and sudden drops made my mouth go dry. I shook my head. "No way."

Before I could protest again, Jim was nudging me toward a line. "You'll have fun," he said. "Don't be a wuss."

Mom stayed back to watch with Brittany as I walked up a set of stairs leading to four slides, each a different color: blue, pink, orange, and green. The slides snaked back and forth, coiling around each other until they dumped riders into a shallow pool. When I got to the front of the line, I read the safety sign. An image showed a person with arms folded and legs crossed.

My coffin.

I stood at the top of the stairs, heart racing. The sharp smell of chlorine burned my nostrils, but before I could rub my nose to relieve the pain, a Geauga Lake employee standing beside me blew a whistle.

"Yikes!" I jumped and grabbed the plastic railing.

"Go!" he shouted.

"Go?" I asked.

"Yes, go!"

So, scared as I was, I bit my lip, sat down in the pink slide, and pushed off. I swished back and forth. Each time I hit a bump, my folded arms and crossed ankles flew spread-eagle, causing me to swish closer to the lip of the slide. I hated Jim for making me ride that death trap.

At some point I almost got the hang of it, but then the slide ended, and the water ejected me into the pool of rushing water, which crammed my neon pink and green leopard swimsuit between my butt cheeks to the point of mild pain. I stopped for a moment and yanked the wedgie out.

Someone blew another whistle. I gazed up to see a lifeguard with shiny sunglasses and spiked hair looking down at me from the side of the pool. "Unload from the pool area!"

"Sorry. Jeez." I walked through the water as fast as I could and exited the pool using the steps.

We met back up with the rest of the family and walked to the picnic area. My wet swimsuit kept sneaking up between my cheeks and my soggy, stone-washed jean shorts made picking the wedge difficult. I wiggled and writhed.

For lunch we had fountain sodas brimming with ice and crispy fries with a side of warm vinegar for dipping.

"How about the wave pool?" asked Aunt Beatrice.

"Sounds fun," said Trina.

"I can handle that," I said. But I didn't hear the *wave* part. I thought we were heading to the regular kind of pool.

As we got closer, I immediately knew I was in trouble. It was a massive blue pool with waves cresting at the concrete shore. A crowd of paste-colored bodies bobbed up and down in orange and yellow innertubes. It hardly seemed safe.

"What the heck?" I asked. On the wall at the very end of the pool, a mural of a wave stretched from one side to the other, with two menacing eyes staring at me from its center.

"It's safe, Dani. You'll like it," said Trina, smiling.

After I greased myself up like a pig for the second time, I sat down in the shallow end and splashed with my sister. Over and over, I filled her little neon-colored plastic cups with water and poured them back out, letting the chlorine-filled liquid trickle back out into the pool. Every time, she'd giggle and clap at my trick. At least the ankle-deep water wouldn't compromise my safety and health.

Then an old Band-Aid floated next to me.

"Yuck," I said, scooting away.

"Will you please come in with me?" Trina begged. I noticed she was wearing one of her three new bikinis. Uncle Matt worked for one of the big computer companies and her mom liked to spend money. Trina always had new stuff.

"Come on, Danielle! Get in here with us!" Aunt Beatrice shouted from the deeper water, waving around an orange tube to get my attention.

"But I can't swim," I muttered.

"Everyone can swim, Danielle. Don't be a chicken," Trina said.

"Go on," said Mom. She was sitting next to me in her classic black swimsuit. "You know she won't stop until you listen to her." Mom and Aunt Beatrice were best friends. I had seen pictures of them from the seventies, and they looked like two brunette bombshells with tiny waists and perfect hair. "Watch her, Jim," Mom said as she twisted the gold rings around her fingers.

"I will," he grumbled back.

I rolled my eyes and trudged through the water with Jim and Trina until I reached Aunt Beatrice.

"It'll be fun." She laughed and handed me the orange ring. "Let's make a human chain."

Kids sat inside the tubes and adults held onto the handles. We floated along until we reached the sign that read "8 feet" and waited for the big wave: six of us with three tubes. Uncle Matt still had his glasses on, and that made me giggle.

The alarm sounded, signaling that the big wave was coming, and I thought I might puke. It wasn't a friendly sounding alarm. More like a get-out-of-the-water-if-you-give-two-craps-about-your-safety kind of alarm.

I wrapped my arms around the orange ring and squeezed tight.

"Why did I agree to this?" I asked. No one answered.

I couldn't get out fast enough to avoid the wave, so I closed my eyes and braced for it. The swell of water pushed from behind me, and I knew it was too strong. We were too close to the end and the wave was far too big. Someone let go of my ring, and it capsized. Water rushed over me, filling my mouth, ears, and bathing suit. I went head over feet, over head, over feet again. My arms and legs flailed as the water engulfed me. My chest tightened. Holding my breath grew harder to do as the seconds dragged on.

I careened through the water, bubbles tickling my arms and legs, bodies touching me, then nothing but water. My hands and feet thrashed and grabbed, but my fingers kept coming up empty. I thought that would be how I died: in a pool with hundreds of overweight, suburban, white families bobbing around in a germ-infested wave pool. They'd find me face-down with a wedgie.

Before I could get my bearings and come up for air, something hard connected with my head. For a moment I heard nothing, saw nothing, felt nothing. I blacked out. Then a breeze tickled my ear and jolted me to a standing position. Discombobulated, I didn't understand how the water only reached my calves. A lifeguard rushed over and asked if I was okay.

"You hit heads with that guy over there." She pointed to a man with a bowling ball belly sitting in a foot of water, rubbing his head. Another lifeguard crouched to talk to him. Poor guy. Even the shallow end wasn't safe.

Mom rushed over with my sister in her arms. "Danielle! You went sailing with the wave! You could have drowned." The rest of my family plodded through the water towards me.

"Are you sure you're okay?" the lifeguard repeated.

I coughed. "I'm not sure." I rubbed my head. "But I think so."

After that, someone announced over the loudspeaker that they had to shut down the wave pool due to a possible concussion. We found an empty table, and I yanked my shorts back on over my soaking suit.

Despite a throbbing temple, I felt normal, but the lifeguards monitored me, and someone brought me banana split Dippin' Dots ice cream. After a half-hour, they released me and re-opened the death pool.

"Why don't we take it easy for the rest of the day?" Mom asked, pushing the stroller through the park.

"I'd like that." I smiled and linked my arm through hers.

"Games?" asked Aunt Beatrice, checking her wallet.

"Yeah!" Trina and I shouted together, then giggled.

We found the arcade, and Stan won a four-foot-tall pink tiger in the water gun race and gave it to Trina.

"Where's mine?" I joked with Jim.

He laughed and belched from too much pop. "Win it yourself."

After about an hour, Aunt Beatrice said, "Well guys, I think it's time to go."

Nobody argued. We'd had enough American excess for one vacation. Trina and Stan carried the tiger together through the never-ending lines of minivans and sedans, weaving back and forth until we found our parking spots.

"Where are the keys?" asked my aunt, tugging on her van's locked door. Everyone patted their pockets and shrugged.

"I think they might be in the console." Stan cringed. As I watched the sweat drip off Aunt Beatrice and Uncle Matt, seeing Trina and Stan struggle with the stupid pink tiger, I felt strangely satisfied.

"Should we go back to the pool?" I joked.

Jim lit a cigarette and snorted.

The Slumber Party[2]

I met Debra on my first day of seventh grade. With jitters racing through my heart, I walked into class early, pulled out my school supplies, and doodled to distract my hands from shaking. Second in the classroom, Debra slid into the seat next to me with casual ease.

"Hey!" She smiled at me, yanking her folder and spiral notebook from her backpack. She tossed them on the desk and started clicking her pen.

"Hey." *Be cool, be normal,* I reminded myself. Attempting to be nonchalant, I dropped my pen on my desk and waved.

"I'm Debra," she said. "What's your name?" We could have been cousins with our pale skin, freckles, and long brown hair.

"Danielle," I said, speaking slowly so I wouldn't trip over my words.

"Cool. Wanna eat lunch with me?" She tucked a loose strand of hair behind her ear and tilted her head sideways.

"Yeah, sure." I smiled back.

I couldn't get used to the transition from being in one class all day in elementary school to switching classrooms for every subject. There were two parts of the school (old and new) and strange hallways that intersected, with rooms numbered differently on each side. I got lost twice and never did find the rooftop pool the eighth graders raved about.

At lunch, I was relieved to see a familiar face. Debra and I talked nonstop. We realized we both had younger siblings, moms who worked hard, and no money to buy nice things. Before I finished my peanut butter sandwich, the bell rang.

"What do you have next?" Debra asked, leaning over my shoulder to look at my class schedule. We left the lunchroom together, side by side.

---

2 A version of this essay was published in *The Passed Note*.

"Looks like science. Room 203," I said.

"Me too!" She bounced from foot to foot.

It was a little too early to call it, but I thought I'd found my BFF.

A few months later, Debra tossed me a note in homeroom folded up like a triangle with a smiley face drawn on the front. I waited until the teacher turned to write on the blackboard before I opened it. The note said, *I know it's cheesy, but I'm having a sleepover this weekend for my birthday. Wanna come?*

I glanced over and smiled at her, nodding.

Later, at lunch, I said, "I haven't been to a sleepover in forever. Who else is coming?"

"Just some friends. It'll be great," Debra said, looking at her foam plate. She seemed distracted by her lunch.

That weekend, on the way to the slumber party, Mom asked, "Do you know these girls?" She was worried about me. I could tell by the way her knuckles whitened from gripping the steering wheel too tight.

She drove past my old elementary school and the playground where I'd once peed my pants. I had been standing by the swings, and I couldn't hold it. A warm geyser had burst from my dress onto the dirt beneath me. But we had been only six, and my classmates quickly forgot all about it.

"No, but I'll be fine. It's just one night." I offered her a thin smile. As a preteen, I missed being young without worry.

Mom pulled up to Debra's house, a modest bungalow on Upton Street, two blocks from junior high. Several girls from the in-crowd congregated on the front lawn. I wondered why those girls were there; Debra and I weren't cool. We were the poor kids.

All the girls wore crisp Nike shirts, pressed jeans, and matching sneakers. I looked down at my only pair of good jeans and the hole forming on the knee. It would be years before ripped jeans were fashionable, and Mom didn't have money to buy me a new pair. She folded and stocked women's clothes at a discount store, and Jim repaired boat motors at a marina up in Michigan, thirty minutes away. His job barely covered the gas it took for him to ride his motorcycle back and forth. Without hand-me-downs from teenage cousins and neighbors, I would have been wearing jeans off the clearance rack from the store where Mom worked. No-name jeans never fit right. They were too short, too tight, too sparing in the crotch.

"Call me, okay?" said Mom, twisting and twirling her rings. I looked up to see her eyes searching my face for assurance.

"I'll be fine," I told her. *I'll be fine*, I repeated to myself. But the thought of spending an entire night in a room full of girls I barely knew made my knees tremble.

Debra smiled at me from the middle of the crowd, waving.

"Love you." I squeezed my mom's arm, pecked her on the cheek, climbed out of the car, and shut the door.

"Love you too," she said through the window. Then she drove away and turned the corner before I focused my attention back on the girls. *Act normal*. I slung my bag over my shoulder, careful not to drop my new TLC CD. I had used money from my piggy bank to buy it at the mall. The flawless plastic, the fresh paper, the gleaming disc: all of it represented weeks of chores done around the house and the time I babysat my cousins while my aunt and uncle went bowling. Nice things didn't just fall into my lap. Being normal was expensive.

After greeting my friend and the other girls, careful to avoid too much eye contact, we walked through her front door. Inside, Debra's mom sat on a broken-in brown couch eating a grilled cheese sandwich and watching the small television in the corner. The rabbit ears needed to be adjusted. Static rippled through the screen, but she seemed content with the picture.

"Hi, Debra's mom," I said.

"Hey girls. Have fun," she muttered without looking up.

We walked through the tiny kitchen. Dirty pots and pans spilled out of the sink onto the counters. Debra had two younger siblings, and her mom worked long hours.

Debra's room was in the basement, with spiders who spun webs high in the corners. Her mom ran out of room on the first level for another bedroom, so Debra took a corner of the unfinished space and added posters to the wall to make it her own. It had a cement floor and smelled like damp clothes, but at least she had privacy.

Downstairs, we tossed our backpacks and sleeping bags on the floor and sat in a circle near the dryer. We warmed up to each other with a game of Truth or Dare. Most of it was innocent: the truth about a first kiss; a dare to prank-call an ex. I listened and laughed but mostly stewed in my own thoughts. *Am I fitting in? Can they tell I'm nervous? Can they tell I'm poor?*

"Truth or dare, Danielle?" Carla asked, startling me from my thoughts. She was a pretty Mexican girl with curly brown hair that fell to her hips and new sneakers on her feet at least every other month. I didn't know Carla at all, didn't have classes with her or ride the bus with her, but I knew *of* her from the hallway. She was always surrounded by her popular friends.

"Um, truth, I guess." My cheeks simmered.

"Okay. Tell me 'bout David."

"Oh, um . . . I dated him for like two weeks. Didn't work out." David was an almost-famous boxer, a jock *everyone* wanted to date, who remained my friend after our two-week dating trial, which consisted of only a few phone calls and one dance in the school gym.

"Whatever." Carla sneered, shrugging her shoulders and rolling her eyes. "This game is boring. Let's do something else." She looked to Nicole, a pint-sized blond with glasses whom I'd only seen at lunch making fun of the band kids.

Everyone else turned and stared at me. Six sets of eyes burned holes in my dwindling self-esteem. I stared back at Debra, and she turned her focus to the ground.

"How about music?" Nicole asked. She snatched my TLC CD from the top of my backpack. "Is this yours?" She looked at me.

"Yeah. J-just got it," I sputtered.

Nicole examined both sides of the red case. "You like TLC?"

Puke burned my throat. I didn't trust her, and I needed the uncomfortable fog in the room to lift so I could breathe. "They're pretty good," I said.

She opened the case and looked at Carla. The two of them laughed. Then she bent my CD, cracking it with a *pop*.

"What the hell?" I jumped up but restrained myself from pushing her.

She broke the disc into more pieces with *snaps* and *cracks*. She bent and broke it until shards of iridescent plastic covered the raw basement floor. She ripped the red paper, the words, the pictures, and tossed them up like confetti. Carla, Nicole, all the girls—*even Debra*—laughed. My whole face blazed.

I grabbed my backpack and sleeping bag and stumbled back up the worn wooden steps, where Debra had once told me I was her very best friend. I ran my hand along the rough cinderblock wall for balance.

At the top, I clenched my jaw and stifled a sob.

I swallowed the only crumb of pride I had left and walked into the kitchen. Debra's mom was still sitting on the couch, empty plate beside her, watching a static-filled sitcom with canned laughter. "I n-need a phone," I said. The veneer in my voice cracked, just like my CD.

"Sure. Is everything okay?" Her eyebrows arched in concern.

I knew better than to tattle. If I told her the truth, the rest of junior high would be hell. Girls don't bully with fists as much as boys, but it can be worse. They steal your things, make up rumors, call you names, and play tricks on you.

"I just want to go home."

Grandma Pink

Grandma was a firecracker until the day she died. She always painted her nails fuchsia, even in her seventies. Her skin, soft and thin between each wrinkle, smelled like baby lotion and Freedent Gum. She always had a wild cherry Luden's tucked beneath a crumpled tissue in the pocket of her pastel pink sweater, which she would stuff in my hand with a wink when my mom wasn't looking. I thought I was getting a real treat.

She wore lipstick and fur-lined coats to the grocery store, swore like a sailor, and told me that cookies and milk were an acceptable substitute for dinner, as long as I didn't tell Mom.

During her last years at the upscale assisted living facility where my mom also worked, Grandma got her kicks stealing Oreos off the dessert cart for Brittany and me. From the laundry room, she'd swipe clothes with names like Fanny Mae or Matilda Jean stitched into the collar and give them to my mom. And she insisted we take at least one roll of single-ply toilet paper from her shared bathroom every time we visited. Grandma was Robin Hood with a cane. She took from rich old ladies and gave to her poor family.

Before Mom moved her there, Grandma lived with us for a couple years. Though she mostly watched soap operas in her blue velvet rocking chair, on occasion she'd call a cab to drive us to Big Lots for discounted Cabbage Patch Kids and orange cream soda pop. Mom said her ass was on fire; she couldn't sit still even when the years started to catch up.

Aside from my sister and me, the only things she cared about were *The Young and the Restless*, *The Bold and the Beautiful*, shopping, and Elvis. Mostly Elvis and his swaying hips. In her mind, he was a king. She knew every record word for word and owned every one of his movies. She loved him more than she loved Grandpa. Each year, she celebrated his birthday and mourned the anniversary of his death. She kept his obituary in her jewelry box, but part of her believed he was alive on some remote island because *The National Enquirer* said it was true. Some days we couldn't convince her otherwise.

Her duplex sat on Lagrange Street, in the heart of Toledo's poorest neighborhood. She stayed there, in the neighborhood where she had been born and raised, even when it wasn't a safe place anymore. Shootings and stabbings happened almost every day on her block, but she'd go damned or dead before she'd let her kids sell it. Even after she moved into the assisted living facility, she rented it out to a family friend instead of putting it on the market.

Before she lived with us, and when she was well enough to care for herself, we'd watch wrestling together on the big faux wood television, rooting for our favorites like the Macho Man and Hulk Hogan. One time she even took me to a WWF event at the Toledo Sports Arena and I got to see Jake the Snake wrestle live. I can still smell the dripping sweat and buttery popcorn after all these years.

⌒

I insisted on going to see my grandmother one last time after she passed away, even though Mom tried to convince me I shouldn't. I didn't believe it was true: even at seventy-six, Grandma was too wild to leave me.

In the hospital, I stared at her lifeless body, cheeks sunken and thin lips gaping from her last breath. I kissed the skin on her forehead one last time.

Even then, her nails were perfectly pink.

Unfair Treatment

After eighth grade one day, I walked the half-block home from the bus stop to find an empty driveway. That meant Mom was off running errands somewhere, and Jim was at work. Few situations excited me more than the chance to be home alone—no one to harass me for talking on the phone too much, leaving my laundry on the stairs, or ignoring my Algebra homework.

Mom's note on the counter confirmed her whereabouts and reminded me to watch my sister when she came home from elementary school. *Don't forget to do the dishes,* she added. I glanced at the crusty stacks of plates in the sink and scoffed.

Doing dishes stunk, but supervising Brittany was close to impossible. The kid was a handful. Not a *bad* kid, per se, just a curious climber. At one year old, she'd figured out how to escape her crib and scoot down the flight of stairs to the baby gate, where she'd sit and bawl. Brittany's compulsion to escape only increased as she grew. The previous Easter, when she was about six, she had scaled the chain-link fence in her new Velcro roller skates and fell headfirst onto the other side of our concrete driveway. Mom ran outside when she heard her cry, then scooped her up and took her inside to the couch. Mom asked her why she'd done it, but before Brittany could respond, she spewed the yellow Peeps she'd eaten earlier.

I threw Mom's note in the trash and looked in the fridge for a snack. It was empty aside from condiments and Jim's egg salad. He had recently shown us how to make his perfect version of it. We watched him boil the eggs for ten minutes. After they cooled in an ice bath, we peeled them one by one and placed them into a bowl. Jim mashed them with a fork while Brittany looked on, leaning her head on his shoulder. I stood on the other side of him, a foot away, asking questions to show interest.

"What are the ingredients?"

"Miracle Whip, mustard, salt, and pepper," he said, spooning dollops of Miracle Whip into the egg.

"How much of each?" I asked.

"I eyeball everything." He shrugged and stirred the mixture together, not once looking up from the bowl.

"Can I have the first sandwich, Daddy?" Brittany asked, batting her thick eyelashes at him.

"Course you can, Pudge." He turned his head from the bowl to smile at her, and a sour pang of jealousy hit my gut.

⤚

I heard the front door fling open and the screen door slam shut. "Danielle?" Brittany called.

"In the kitchen."

"Where's Mom?" she asked. She walked up beside me, dropped her backpack on the floor, and eyed my egg salad sandwich. "Ooh. Make me one?"

"Running an errand. I'll split it with you. Grab a knife and plate."

Brittany dragged the other barstool over to the cupboard to reach the plates, small fingers straining to reach the highest shelf. She looked nothing like me. I was leggy with freckles and inky hair. She was short with coppery skin and light hair. Somehow, we both looked like Mom. She climbed back down and handed me the knife and plate, and I cut my sandwich in half to share with her.

"Thanks," she said, taking a bite. I bit into mine too, savoring the sweet saltiness of it.

"Can I go outside?" Brittany asked after she finished her half.

"Wait until Mom gets home. Do your homework or something."

She rolled her eyes.

I grabbed our plates and headed to the sink. "Unless you want to dry?" I said, turning to toss her the drying towel. But she'd already slipped away. I watched her round the corner and march toward the stairs with her too-big backpack bouncing on her shoulder. "Never mind." *Guess I'll be doing the dishes alone, as usual.*

I shifted my attention back to the dishes, quickly washing, rinsing, and loading them onto the rack. After a few minutes, I finished and wiped my hands on the towel. I almost called my new friend Kate that I'd met at lunch, but then I remembered I was watching Brittany. I headed upstairs.

She wasn't in her room. Her backpack lay forgotten on the floor, items from inside strewn about. "Come out, come out, wherever you are," I called. I checked her closet and under the bed. Nothing. I hurried down the stairs, hoping to find her plopped in front of the TV. I checked behind every door, under every table. I ran to the backyard, my panic rising. "Brittany!" I hollered. No response. I ran into the street and looked both ways as far as I could see. No trace of her. My heart sank. Jim's perfect egg salad threatened to come back up like Brittany's Peeps as I stood, paralyzed, wondering what to do. *Should I get my bike and go looking for her?* If I left, and she came back while I was searching, she'd be home alone. Mom might understand, but if Jim came home to find her there without me, I'd be dead.

Just then I saw Jim pull into the driveway. Why couldn't it have been Mom to come home first? Mom understood that Brittany was an escape artist. I paced on the sidewalk, working on an excuse. There wasn't one. Even though Brittany was the one who'd left, I'd be nailed for it. I was the oldest. She was Jim's baby.

I ran in the front door as Jim walked in the back, humming some song and jingling his keys. He tossed them on the counter and opened the fridge.

"Where's your ma?" He cracked open a Pepsi and took a sip. Then he set the can on the counter and adjusted his Harley Davidson t-shirt over his belly.

"Running an errand," I said. I stood there motionless, arms limp at my sides.

"So, where's your sister?" he asked when he turned to face me.

"I don't know." I said, suddenly crying. "She disappeared while I was washing dishes. I looked everywhere for her, I promise."

"God dammit, Danielle." He picked up the phone and dialed Kevin's parents next door. Brittany wasn't there. Then two doors down. They weren't home. Last, he called the neighbors across the street. After a few words, he hung up.

"She's with the twins on a bike ride," he grumbled and raked his hand through his hair. I knew that meant she was either on the handlebars or pegs. Brittany's bike still had training wheels, and even though Mom told her before that riding on the handlebars was dangerous, Brittany loved the thrill.

"Crap," I said, clenching my fists.

Jim headed toward the back door. "I'm going to look for her."

"At least I did the dishes," I muttered.

"Do your homework, smartass," he replied. "You're grounded from the phone for a week."

Before I had the chance to dispute my punishment, he walked away.

Once a Thief

Novembers in Toledo were dark and dreary. This Saturday in particular was no different. Temperatures had fallen from crisp to "crap, it's friggin' freezing." Dark clouds and high winds had settled over our city for the season.

Because of the frigid air outside and our bad insulation inside, Jim had a fire going in our wood-burning stove with wood scraps from the backyard and old newspapers from the neighbor. Brittany had plopped herself in front of the television to watch reruns of *Full House*, munch on knock-off Doritos, and sip Sierra Mist from the can with a neon bendy straw. Brittany loved those Olson girls and bendy straws, as I'm sure most seven-year-old girls did at the time. I only watched because I had a crush on Uncle Jesse.

Mom stopped her needlework to look at me, freshly fourteen, full of angst and bored out of my damn mind.

"Wanna go to Meijer?" She asked. Meijer was a mega-sized store with everything from groceries to electronics and discount clothes. It was a boring place to spend a Saturday, but better than my current situation on the couch.

"Sure," I said. There was a new CD I wanted. Not to hang with my mom or to help her budget our weekly menu. "Coolio has a new single out," I added. What I *really* wanted was to steal something.

"You have money?" she asked.

"Yes," I lied. Until that point, I'd only taken Bonne Bell Dr. Pepper lip gloss and Designer Imposters U from Target. I liked the thrill of being bad, liked the feeling of having some kind of otherwise unaffordable luxury at my fingertips. Shoplifting was cool in junior high, and after the slumber party at Debra's, I tried desperately to fit in with my peers.

But other kids at school stole way better than me. They swiped Nike shirts and Levi jeans from Dillard's when their parents dropped them off at the mall on the weekends. It wasn't fair. Those kids already had nice things. If anyone deserved to steal, it was me.

Right?

As soon as we rushed through the doors of the massive retail chain with chill in our bones, we parted ways. Mom thought she was helping by giving me freedom. She had no idea.

My feet moseyed to the music section, where I pondered my approach and went back and forth about my decision. Mom wouldn't buy it. No extra money. I knew stealing was bad, but my id told me I *needed* it. I skimmed through the new releases for a while before I got the courage to finally shove the disc in my pocket. My right hand worked on ripping the cellophane while I occasionally flipped through the posters with my left.

I glanced over my shoulder on the sly. Behind me, there was suddenly a lady with feathered hair tamed beneath a Detroit Red Wings cap. She was reading the back of Mariah Carey's newest album. *Crap.*

I left the aisle with the CD still in my pocket. The stubborn plastic wouldn't tear, and the magnetic security strip was stuck.

I ducked into the Hallmark aisle. Rows of paper apologies, thank yous, and celebrations in neat order lined both sides. There wasn't a piece of paper there that could save me from the mess I was close to. I turned. Detroit Red Wings lady had followed, and she stood there seemingly distracted by the birthday cards. But I knew better. I'd heard of people like her. She had to be a loss prevention agent, and I was about to get snagged.

My heart raced, face flushed. I walked faster, out of the cards. Weaving, thinking, weighing the consequences of my impending actions. I had desired a bit of naughtiness under my belt, not criminal status. That wasn't me.

In the shoe aisle, I dumped the still-wrapped disc on top of a pair of work boots.

That's when I jogged, almost sprinted but not enough to draw attention, until I found Mom bagging oranges in the produce section on the other side of the store.

"Hey, Mom," I said.

"Find that CD?" she asked, examining a piece of fruit.

"Yeah," I shrugged. "But I can't afford it."

Escape Plan

I woke to warm, gooey air smothering me, even though the ceiling fan was spinning on high. The fan swayed and groaned, ready to jump from its screws in the drywall any second.

I looked at my alarm clock. *One forty-five.* No doubt everyone in my family was sleeping: Jim on the couch with the remote resting in his hand, Mom in her room with her reading glasses still on her nose, and Brittany at a friend's.

Moonlight seeped between tree branches and into my only bedroom window. Throughout the week, because of the rush to get ready for school—and my laziness—my clothes were strewn about in piles on the floor. I sighed. *Mom is gonna make me clean tomorrow.*

Anxious and unable to return to sleep, I tossed the sheets onto the floor with the rest of the mess. I swung my bare legs over the bed, and my foot kicked a box of maxi pads. I wished I could throw that stupid box across the room. That year, I had finally started my period. I remember looking forward to it for so long, but when it showed up as a puddle of red in my favorite underwear, and Mom handed me a package of massive, store-brand pads, I knew it was literally the worst thing that had ever happened to me.

I glanced outside my second-floor window. Just past the edge of the porch roof, the locust tree and its long seed pods hung still. Light from the moon gave the whole scene a bluish tint. There wasn't so much as a stray cat wandering in the gray glow of the cracked concrete street. I wanted to be part of it instead of sitting in my sticky room, wanted to climb outside and get some fresh air on the roof. But if anyone caught me, I'd get grounded for sure.

Whatever.

I pulled the screen out—the removable one Jim bought because mine got ripped away in a thunderstorm—and my heart hammered in my chest.

I stepped through the window and sat. The shingles scraped my legs like sandpaper, so I curled them up to my chest, using my bare feet as stability against the gentle decline. Sitting perched out there felt easy and free.

Streetlights illuminated spots on the gray streets, making shapes like full silver moons. Thin shadows crept between them, swelling into giants.

I could see the ends of the block in both directions. The street was empty and quiet until a car swerved toward me in the distance to the right, the engine grumbling low. I knew it was my neighbor, Gene, from the way his headlights danced clumsily back and forth from one side of the street to the other.

He was likely drunk again. He was always drinking. His car came to an abrupt stop across the street from me, in front of his house, one tire on the curb. When he opened the door, he fell out.

He climbed to his feet, rocked back and forth, jingled his keys, and slammed his car door shut. He stumbled inside, and quiet returned to the street.

In that house, Gene's son Travis was visiting from Florida. Mom said I wasn't allowed to hang out with him. Travis had long hair, he surfed, and he had a reputation for being bad, like his dad. All my new teenage hormones liked that boy. We hung out in his basement sometimes while Mom worked.

A thought entered my mind: *Climb off the roof and run.* But to where? *Maybe across the street.* To do what? I had no clue. But before I could talk any sense into myself, I turned over on my belly to shimmy feet-first to the edge.

I wanted to find the corner of the roof where the twisty iron rod connected the porch floor to the ceiling. If I could find those supports, I could lower myself down it like a ladder. I wiggled and inched along the roof as sweat beaded on my forehead. I paused to take one last look at my window and listen for movement inside. All clear. My toes were inches from the edge.

Then I thought about what it would be like coming back: climb back up the iron posts and scaling the roof. I thought about the possibility of Jim or Mom waking. I imagined someone seeing me: a neighbor who would tattle, or maybe the boy across the street. Whether or not I wanted to admit it, I already knew he was going to break my heart at the end of the summer.

I exhaled defeat and turned onto my hands and knees, crawling like the child I was back toward the window. I slipped inside and secured my screen back in its place. I gathered the sheets from my floor, smelling the lavender detergent. I lay in bed and smoothed my blankets over my dirty knees. In the dark, I could see the silhouettes of the figurines Mom had painted for me when I was young, resting on my shelf like always.

I squeezed my eyes shut and pulled my favorite stuffed koala close. At the moment, that was enough.

Toilet Paper Maché

We met on the corner of a street six blocks from mine, just a few feet shy of a small brick rancher: Cassy's house. We stayed in the shadows, careful to avoid the light from the streetlights. Even though summer vacation had begun two weeks before, a chill lingered in June nights in Ohio that year, so we wore our spartan mascot hoodies—like a trio of idiots wanting to get caught.

"Where's Steve?" I whispered to Chrystal.

"Think he bailed?" asked Jan, taking a hit from her glass bowl. She had been a friend on and off since kindergarten and lived one block over from Cassy. She flicked her tongue piercing against her teeth, and it made a soft *click, click, click.*

Throughout sophomore year, I toilet-papered at least ten houses. Most of them were four-roll jobs: toss a couple in a tree, wrap a couple bushes, maybe even get the car. My new friend, Chrystal, and I stole rolls from our parents' bathrooms and toilet-papered our friends' parents' houses in the middle of the night, usually after Friday night football games.

Cassy's house was different.

"Hey guys," a male voice whispered from behind us.

We turned to find Steve, tall even while slouched on his bike. He rested the mega pack of double-ply on his handlebars. Twenty-four rolls of TP. It would be magnificent.

Our reasons for covering Cassy's house with double-ply were more vindictive than any other time. We weren't playing a joke on a friend. She *wasn't* a friend. She was a total bitch, and we wanted to show her what being a bitch had gotten her. I could hear her in my head, *Like, oh my God, Danielle. Where did you get those shoes? Kmart?* and *You guys can't even buy the good toilet paper?* Plus, she had dumped Steve, one of the few nice guys at our school. We wanted to get her real, *real*, good.

We got to work right away, tossing streams of white into the high branches of Cassy's mature oak trees. They sailed in silence, going up and coming down, going up and coming down. The branches were so high that sometimes the roll wouldn't quite reach, and it would fall back to the ground making a *thwoop* sound.

Steve wrapped an entire roll around the body of the car and up the antenna, leaving a bit at the end to dangle like a white flag. I layered it on the bushes. We even wrapped rolls around the perimeter of the house because there wasn't a fence; just an open, square plot of land with a small ranch-styled house in the center.

Cassy's dad slept on a recliner in front of the television in the living room the entire time we toilet-papered. The curtains hung wide open, and his face reflected a funny shade of blue from the TV. I kept checking to make sure he didn't wake, but he never even flinched. He reminded me of my stepdad, with his hair disheveled, remote slipping from his hand, and potato chips resting on his middle-aged belly. Remorse wiggled into my head, but I ignored it. Half the toilet paper remained.

At the end of our job, we marveled at our white masterpiece. "There is something so peaceful about streams of TP blowing in the summer breeze," said Jan through a cloud of pot smoke.

"Her parents are gonna be so pissed." I laughed.

Steve laughed and combed his hands through his hair. "I wonder if Cassy will have to clean—"

Before he could finish his sentence, raindrops fell. Big fat ones splatted on my head, slow at first, drizzling. In an instant it switched to a downpour, pelting and soaking us.

"Shit, guys! We gotta go!" Chrystal said.

I nodded, and we bolted six blocks in the summer rain. At her street, the one before mine, we hugged.

"Good job tonight," she said. Nervous laughter spilled from her mouth.

"Oh man." I shook my head in disbelief. "See you tomorrow?"

"Tomorrow."

I snuck into my parents' house, dripping wet, and went straight to bed with a smile on my face. I wondered what would happen to the toilet paper. Would it stick or fall to the ground?

The following day, Chrystal and I rode our bikes to Cassy's house and found her dad out front, hunched on his hands and knees, scraping dried-up white bits off the stoop with a metal paint scraper. Toilet paper clung to the trees, the bushes, to everything. Like paper maché.

He paused when he saw us gawking at the house out of his peripheral vision. "Hey girls." He offered a sheepish wave before scratching his still-disheveled hair and turning his attention to the bushes next to the front door. Bit by bit, he untangled the toilet paper.

I thought about Mom and Jim, and how I'd feel if they had to clean up a mess like that. Cassy's dad probably worked the line at one of our local factories, long shifts through the week to make ends meet—and now, because of us, he was working on his day off. I looked over to Chrystal, wide-eyed. She swallowed hard.

"Let's go," I whispered. We peddled away.

Sticky Notes

Our tiny house would have been in shambles had Mom not managed it with the precision of a surgeon. She swept the floors twice daily, hand-washed the dishes to a pristine shine, and folded my stepdad's holey socks, grease-stained shirts, and skid-marked underwear into perfect squares.

When I was in my late teens, Mom also worked ten-hour shifts as a hospice aid, wiping old butts. Before that, she folded and stocked women's clothes at a discount clothing store. And before that, she was the night manager at Video Connection and brought home life-size cutouts of Dick Tracy and Roger Rabbit. Mom worked hard.

She also attended every home varsity basketball game so she could watch me dance, and every football game to see Brittany twirl her flag. For dance competitions, she made matching bows for all my teammates.

Once my mother's mother and father had both died, she put everything she had into us, her job, and the house on Custer Drive to keep herself busy. But she wasn't great at delegating chores—or maybe we just refused to listen to her. I would rummage through the pantry for pretzels and Pop-Tarts, forgetting to close the cabinet and leaving a trail of crumbs that led to the couch. Jim would leave cups half-filled with milk starting to spoil on the living room end table and used undershirts balled up in the corner of the bathroom floor next to his wet towels. Brittany never filled the toilet paper when she emptied it. She'd rest the new roll on top of the old cardboard tube.

Often, Mom yelled at us. She ripped the phone cord from the wall after I dragged it into the bathroom to talk to my friends one too many times, threw bills into the air, chain-smoked her menthol light one hundred cigarettes, and cried. She cried so much, but I didn't know how to stop it.

This lack of respect or help continued for years, until one otherwise normal day when I walked in from the bus stop two long blocks away, seventeen and too lazy to get my license. I tossed my backpack in the middle of the living room floor next to one of our three miniature Lhasa Apso dogs and bent to rub her belly. That's when I noticed the first note in the corner of my vision, stuck to a case on top of the DVD player.

Put away after viewing.

"Huh?"

I stood and walked into the kitchen, at the time decorated in Mom's latest kitchen craze: apples. In the midst of all the red fruit, yellow notes with a permanent marker scribbled on them clung to everything: *Don't leave me open* on the pantry cupboard door; *Throw me away after you drink me* on the milk inside the fridge; and *Don't leave your junk here* on the counter, cluttered with unpaid bills.

In the bathroom, *Replace me when empty* was above the wooden toilet paper holder and *Flush me* was stuck to the toilet's cracked seat.

Take things up with you sat on the steps next to a pile of my clean clothes.

"Mom lost it," I whispered. But before finding her, I reconsidered my decision to drop my crap in the living room and jogged back to grab it. I scooped up a pile of clothes on my way upstairs and placed them on my unmade bed.

"Mom?" I hollered.

"In here." Her voice carried in from her bedroom, the room next to mine.

I found her clipping hot rollers into her long hair in the master bath, a cloud of smoke surrounding her, a cigarette sat burning in the filled ashtray on the back of the toilet.

"Where are you going?" I asked.

"Out for dinner with Dad," she said, smearing mulberry lipstick across her lips.

"On a date?" They never went out. Especially not on school nights.

"Yes. A date." She combed mascara along her eyelashes, applied rouge to her cheeks. "You'll keep an eye on your sister. We won't be out long. I need some . . . time."

"You okay?"

"Yep. Just great. Why?" Mom sprayed a bit of patchouli perfume on her wrists.

"Oh, you know . . . the yellow notes. They're everywhere." I gestured toward the stairs outside her bedroom door.

"Those? Oh, nope. Just tired of yelling."

Presence: Part II

I was at work, slathering garlic butter onto breadsticks with something that resembled a paintbrush, when my biological father, Don, decided to drop in and see me for my eighteenth birthday. It had been ten years since I'd last seen him.

At the time, I worked at an Italian fast-food place called Fettuccine's. The day he came back to Toledo, I had already chopped mountains of lettuce and tomatoes, put together piles of sub sandwiches, and stirred gallons of sauces. A red plastic apron protected my work shirt, except for the burned spot on the apron belly where someone had gotten too close to the oven. I had sauce in my hair and on my shirt. I smelled like roasted garlic.

My boss, a mousy woman with frizzy blond hair whose nerves frazzled easily, came back to tell me he was there. "Danielle, some guy out there says he's your dad." She twisted a rogue curl to the side of her head and looked over her shoulder toward the dining room. "I met your dad before, and it ain't him."

I dropped my butter brush and looked past her through the food service window. There he stood, with long gray hair tucked beneath a dingy trucker hat. His tall, slender stature was the same, but wrinkles had replaced the soft cheeks I remembered.

"Want me to send him away?"

"No. I'll take care of it." I huffed and walked out of the kitchen.

I stopped in the supply room to hang up my apron and catch my breath. Then I wiped butter from my forehead and clenched both fists before trudging to the register.

The counter separated us, but I was close enough to smell the stale smoke on his grease-covered jean jacket—the same jacket he had been wearing on Mom's front porch ten years prior. Even at eight years old, I had already known he would be unreliable. It's a sickening feeling, not being able to trust your own dad.

After the years of girls bullying me, the days when there was almost no food in the fridge, the times when I wondered if my stepdad really loved me like he loved my sister, the times when I wished I had my real father around at least a little . . . I eventually grew to a place where I didn't need him anymore.

"Why are you here?" I asked, stiffening my posture.

"I wanted to see you."

"You can't just show up like this." I knew my eyes were grayish blue like his. I hoped mine weren't as cold and empty. When I stared into them, he looked away.

"I drove all the way from Tennessee to see you." I followed his gaze toward the dining room windows.

Outside, I could see a semi parked in the restaurant's lot. "In your truck, on a delivery? Convenient."

"I hoped we could eat lunch together."

"I don't want to eat lunch with you. Ten years pass without a phone call, and you think you can just come here?" I hid my shaking hands behind the register.

"Do you need new sneakers? I can give you birthday money." He stuffed his hands in his pockets and rocked back on his heels.

I scoffed. "I don't want your money, and I have work to do. Please leave."

I marched back to the supply room with tears stinging my eyes and wondered why he couldn't be a normal father. I put on my red plastic apron and stomped back to my breadsticks in the kitchen. My boss handed me my butter brush. I peered up, meeting her eyes.

"Tell me when he's gone."

"Sure." She clasped her small hand around my shoulder, gentle, yet firm. I wanted to cry, but I didn't. I wouldn't.

My father bought lunch and sat down in the dining room to eat by himself. When he finished, I watched him return his tray and leave.

Nothing a Band-Aid Can't Fix

Six months out of high school, I was still working at Fettuccine's. I had no plans for my future other than the heartburn I knew I'd develop from the buffalo wings I'd just finished devouring with friends. My phone buzzed. I licked the sticky sauce from my fingers, then pulled the phone from my pocket. My boyfriend, Kyle, had texted me.

It's over. Come get your shit.

I glared at the message as tears welled in my eyes. My on-and-off boyfriend of two years dumped me via a text message. I thought my salty boneless wings were about to re-enter the world.

"What's the matter?" Kate asked. She had been my best friend since junior high, after Debra, and she could always see it in my face when something was off. She flipped her black curls over her shoulder and placed her soft hand on my arm. The smell of cocoa butter wafted into my nose. It calmed me enough to tell her.

"It's Kyle. He just broke up with me."

"Again?" asked Chris, Kate's boyfriend at the time. He wiped his hands with a Wet-Nap before scratching his pierced lip.

Chris had been around long enough to know the deal with Kyle and me. I had been seventeen when we started dating. He was twenty-one, making our relationship technically illegal. But that didn't stop me from sneaking out the back door to see him each night. Even worse, Kyle had a child with a woman only one year older than me. For the last couple of months, he just couldn't decide who he wanted to be with.

Looking back, I can't say I blamed him for wanting to make things right with his baby's momma. But that didn't stop the wounds from deepening with each breakup.

"Again." I sighed. "He told me to come get my stuff. Only . . . if Laura is there, this won't be good. She has a temper."

"I'll drive you," said Chris, offering me a thin, hopeful smile.

"And I'll cut a bitch if she tries anything," said Kate. I laughed because I knew she would. She was my ride-or-die, my best friend for life.

We paid our tab and loaded into Chris's muscly black Camaro. Minutes later we turned onto Kyle's street, and my heart started racing. I knew nothing would happen with Kyle; he was all words. But Laura was known for being small and feisty. Once, she threw a cordless phone at Kyle's face and gave him a black eye. He had called the cops, and somehow he was the one who spent the night in jail. I didn't want anything to do with her.

Chris slowed down just before the yellow speed bump sign in front of Kyle's house. *I'm here*, I texted Kyle. Chris rolled down the passenger window, and I looked out from the back seat through a gap between Kate's seatbelt and the car door frame. I breathed in the fresh-cut grass and gasoline fumes from Chris's car and stared at the brick steps leading up to the house, trying to take in everything one last time. The Sunday afternoons spent watching television. The time we'd made out in the pouring rain in his backyard. I decided to hold onto those memories and let go of the other, not-so-good ones. Like the time when he'd been a no-show at my graduation party, or the several times he'd dumped me before.

I waited for his front door to open, for the closure I expected from Kyle. A smile, a nod, maybe even a "See you around." Instead, Laura opened the front door with a jolt, flipped us the bird, and hurled a garbage bag down the steps. It landed in the front yard with a *thud*. The front door slammed, and once again there was nothing but brick steps, fresh-cut grass, and gasoline fumes.

"What the fuck just happened?" asked Chris. I shook my head. What's worse was that I didn't care. I had gone through some version of breaking up and getting back together with Kyle so many times that I was tired of it. I was tired of him.

"Lean forward and let me out, K," I said, tapping on the seat in front of me. Kate did, and as I placed my feet on the street outside, first one and then the other, I felt like I was on solid ground for the first time since high school. Although so many things were still up in the air—college, a career, finding my purpose—at least I no longer had a confused boyfriend stringing me along too. I walked across his front yard, grabbed the garbage bag, and tossed it into Chris's trunk. As I did, I sliced my finger on broken glass sticking out from inside the bag. I stuck my finger in my mouth and sucked, tasting metal. I glanced inside the bag and found my hoodie, a pair of pajamas, and a couple broken picture frames. I picked up one of the photos, now ripped into pieces, and ran my fingers along the rough edge, then tossed everything back in the bag and slammed the trunk shut.

I climbed back in the car and texted Kyle. *This time it's for good.*

"You okay?" asked Kate as she turned her head to look at me.

"Yeah, actually." I smiled. "Nothing a Band-Aid can't fix."

Getting Off Easy[3]

It was close to 10:30 at night when Jan tossed me a second Natty Light. I cracked it open and took a sip. We were sitting in her old Chevy sedan across the street from a shoddy nightclub in downtown Toledo, working on a buzz before going inside.

Twenty-one was two years away, and even though girls got in the club for free, we weren't willing to flirt with older men for drinks. In the front seat, Jan and Amy lit a joint. I cracked my window, and the skunky weed mixed with an old-car exhaust smell. When they handed it to me, I reminded them I didn't smoke weed. It wasn't my thing. Although beer wasn't my thing either, but I drank it anyway, and it bit my throat.

Raindrops the size of marbles bombed the steamed-up windshield, and I wished I'd remembered to bring a jacket. My hairspray wouldn't hold in a downpour. I drew a baby's footprint with the side of my hand in the steam on the window, then another and another between sips of beer. I heard laughter but didn't pay attention to the jokes. I wanted to finish my beer and go dancing.

I gazed up at the ceiling of Jan's car, where thumbtacks held photos of smiling faces: some with friends holding drinks, some with strangers smoking bowls, skipping class senior year, and parties after homecoming. Though I'd known her since kindergarten, I was only in the recent pictures: the ones with sparkles on our cheeks and glow sticks in our hands.

Behind the rain and the laughter, I heard Nelly Furtado singing on the radio about being a bird. I felt just like her, like my father: a girl with good intentions and bad habits who shouldn't be trusted.

"Turn it up. I love this song," I said. Jan cranked the dial on the old

---

3 A version of this essay was originally published in *Beach Reads II: Lost and Found*.

radio, and we joined in with Nelly, singing every word.

I only recently convinced Jan and her best friend to start going out with me. They were my newest group of nightclub friends. Three nights a week, I'd drag them to Main Street in downtown Toledo, or to the fancy Bijou, or to Detroit, an hour north. Just like Chrystal, eventually they'd grow tired of dressing up with me. They'd stay in more. They'd find boys who'd say they loved them and new friends who had their own apartments, so I'd just find a new group to blend with.

I was looking for more than what my family or the bottom of a beer could offer. I was looking for a freedom I'd never touched, for a release I'd only seen in movies; palpable yet still untouchable in the sweat I felt when I brushed against a stranger on the dance floor, when the buzz hit. I was looking for life fulfillment in the wrong places but was too young to know it.

A sudden, bright light shone in my eyes and tapped on the driver's side window. A Toledo cop stood outside the car. I tossed my can on the ground, and Jan cranked the window down to ask the officer how she could help him.

"You ladies have somewhere to be?"

No answer was right. We looked guilty because we were guilty. His flashlight reflected off the empty cans on the floor. The weed smoke clouded up the car and seeped out the window. I wondered if someone would call our parents if we had to go down to the station. I worried that I wouldn't be able to go dancing.

"We were just leaving, sir," said Jan.

The officer frowned and sighed. "Consider this your warning."

Copper and Coffee[4]

At twenty years old, I was certain I wanted to work in marketing and advertising. I imagined getting hired at the agency down the street from my parents' house. It was an angular building with a copper roof. It didn't fit in Toledo between the dilapidated car shop and the canned food factory, but it had always been there on the often-traveled road between my house and the highway.

I daydreamed about what the inside looked like, sure my days would consist of choosing between fonts like Arnhem and Fresco Sans and picking the perfect shade of red for magazine ads. I'd wear pencil skirts with tiny belts and button-down shirts with oversized collars. My hair would be tied back in a no-fuss bun and I'd sit behind a massive acrylic C-shaped desk with an original Salvador Dali on the wall.

I wanted that posh life so bad I could smell the Emporio Armani for Her on my skin.

Chrystal and I had reconnected, and I had moved out to live in a run-down house with her and her cousin, Cody; still near home, but away from my parents' rules. I was broke as hell, but the rent was cheap, and I needed to prove I could make it on my own.

Chrystal and I spent our weekends watching bootleg movies and throwing keggers for friends. I drank too much cheap beer and lost my motivation to get into college. I kept my job at Fettuccine's only to support my drinking and spending habits.

Two years prior, when I had turned eighteen, I scurried to the mall to collect as many credit cards as I could. It only took a year to max them out on clothes for the nightclub and fancy bras to stick in my drawer.

---

4 A version of this essay was originally published in *The Fredericksburg Literary and Art Review.*

One day, I walked into the kitchen of my temporary home. Medallion-shaped yellow and green linoleum tile patterned its way from one end of the kitchen to the other. It was original from the sixties, but not the cool kind of vintage.

"Chrystal, mind if I use your computer?" I asked.

Chrystal was at the old brown stove making Jell-O shots for our next party. "Sure, what for?" she asked, turning toward me.

"Need to update my resumé for this job."

Chrystal had a good job in medical coding. She could afford her truck payment, her insurance, her rent. "Don't want to work at Fettuccine's anymore?" Her eyebrows rose.

"I'm so sick of it." I couldn't stand the smell of garlic anymore. I'd scream if that brick of a drive-through headset fell off my head one more time.

She smiled. "Oh, awesome for you! Want to smoke to celebrate?"

"Nah. You know I don't like pot." I waved my hands.

"Just an offer." She shrugged and walked away with a glass bowl and a bag of green stuff in her hand.

My resumé was unimpressive, but I printed it anyway with a short cover letter and stuffed it into my purse.

The next day, I drove it to the agency on my way to work, wearing my only collared shirt tucked into a gray skirt with black strappy heels.

The foyer floors and walls were black granite, sparkling beneath the second-story vaulted skylights. I gazed around. A massive television played CNN on mute by the entrance on the left, and on the right a spiral steel staircase wound up to the second floor. Enclosed offices with floor-to-ceiling glass doors and walls lined both sides of the building. The employees inside didn't look like what I'd envisioned at an advertising agency. They didn't look special or fancy, just people in work clothes typing, talking on their phones while twirling the phone cords, or snacking on candy and sipping from huge mugs.

Straight in front of me was the receptionist's oval granite desk. It looked big enough to weigh down the rest of the building. Everything smelled like

Xeroxed paper and expensive coffee.

The office was quiet, so I tried to tiptoe to the receptionist, but my in-experienced feet clunked across the floor in my heels.

"Can I help you?" the receptionist asked, bringing her sharp green eyes to meet mine. She was a young blond with a magnetic smile.

"I'd . . ." I swallowed a gulp of air. "I'd like to drop off my resumé." I held up a white envelope that had curled on the edges from being jammed in my bag.

She stood, exposing her almost-due belly. "I'll take that. Thanks."

"Thanks." I turned, waved, and walked out the door.

That weekend Chrystal and I had a colossal party. Every room over-flowed with loud, belligerent people. Smoke of various kinds hovered like a gray fog. Friends slurped down Chrystal's shots in less than an hour.

Some regulars from high school congregated in my bedroom, which was only big enough for a futon and one dresser. Somehow my bedroom ended up being the spot to smoke pot. After my fourth beer, I couldn't stop thinking about my resumé, and how I should've beefed up my high school marketing class experience and educational awards.

"Want a hit?" Chris asked, holding up a small glass bowl.

I grabbed it from him without thinking. "Can you light it for me?"

He lit the end of the bowl and I inhaled, but only a little. The tip burned my lips. I stared down the end of his glass pipe to see him: his bleached hair, wide grin, and pierced face. He laughed. "Holy shit. Dan-ielle smoked." I pulled a seed from my lips and hacked up a string of vio-lent coughs.

The next thing I remember is puking in a stew pot in my bedroom.

"You should get some sleep," someone—I think Kate—said.

My eyes glazed over as I bear-hugged the huge saucepan. "Okay." I ush-ered everyone from my room and passed out to muffled metal music and laughter.

Monday, the owner of the advertising agency called me while I was curled up on the couch watching a bootleg version of *Spiderman* with Chi-nese subtitles.

"Mute that!" I shouted at Chrystal. "It's the advertising agency." She grabbed the remote and hit mute before I answered.

"Hello?" I paced back and forth on the ugly red carpet.

"Hi. Miss Tucker?"

"Speaking."

"This is Mr. Copper from Copper Advertising Agency. We received your resumé at the perfect time. Are you available to interview?"

"Of course. When?" *What if they drug test me?* I bit my lip.

"Tomorrow."

I swallowed hard before responding with a little-too-loud "Sure!" After hanging up the phone, I danced around the living room on the ratty carpet. *One day, I'll have my own place,* I thought, *and it'll have nice floors.*

I used the little cushion I had left on my Express card to buy a new purple button-down with silver stripes. I found it on the clearance rack. It was too big in the sleeves, but I needed the boost of confidence for the interview. New clothing always did that for me.

The owner's office was nothing like I imagined. It was dark with burgundy shades half-drawn, full of oversized mahogany and leather furniture that seemed out of place. The office smelled like cigars and old money. It would have fit better in a chalet or ski lodge.

Mr. Copper was a thin, balding man who wore a pressed white shirt decorated with gold cufflinks. "What kind of experience do you have?" he asked.

"None. But I've dreamt of working here." I kept eye contact and good posture.

He raised an eyebrow, then leaned back in his chair. The leather groaned in response. *He thinks I'm tenacious. Good.*

"Do you know Word and Excel?" he asked.

"Yes." I half-lied. I knew Word. I'd *seen* Excel. Never used it. *How hard can it be?*

"Our receptionist is going on maternity leave. It's temporary."

"I understand."

"Okay, then." He shrugged. "You start next week."

"Wow. Thank y—"

He raised his hand to cut me off. "I get here at nine a.m., and I expect you here before that." He nodded and looked toward the computer. I waited for him to excuse me, watching him type. He looked up, annoyed. "You can leave now," he said.

"Sorry. Thanks for the opportunity." I slunk out of the office before straightening my shoulders and plastering a smile on my face.

Downstairs, I gave a quick wave to the receptionist, who was opening mail. I thought she said, "Good luck. You're gonna need it," but I couldn't be sure because the last part was muffled.

I went straight from my interview to baking breadsticks at Fettuccine's, changing into my uniform in the bathroom before anyone noticed my clothes. I avoided my boss for as long as I could. I stayed in the back and kept my head down toward the metal prep table.

"Is something wrong?" she asked, startling me from slicing sub bread. Her blond hair framed her face in wiry wisps. Even more wiry than usual. She was disheveled after a busy lunch rush, keeping her cool under the pressure of making the perfect pasta for hungry guests.

How do I tell her? "I'm fine. Why?"

"You seem . . . different."

I bit the inside of my cheek. "There is something."

"What is it? I need to do inventory, so make it quick, unless it can wait."

"I need to drop down to weekends for a couple months."

"When?" Her eyes widened.

Shit. Shoulda waited. "Next week." I cringed.

Her inventory clipboard clattered from her hands onto the prep table, and she flapped the collar of her butter-stained Fettuccine's jacket to let in some air. "Why?"

"I got a temp job at the advertising agency." I didn't have to elaborate the name. We only had one in Toledo, and everyone knew it was my dream job.

"I wish you woulda given me more time."

"I'm sorry."

On Monday, I showed up at the agency at 8:30 a.m. expecting to have at least a quick run-down of my duties from the receptionist. Nope. She was already on maternity leave. Instead, she left me a note with instructions under a glass paperweight, and nothing more. *Crap.*

Per her note, I brewed the coffee, collected the mail, watered the plants, turned the television on. Then I waited: for the staff to arrive, for the phone to ring, for requests to be emailed.

At 8:50 a.m., my coworkers started filing in and greeted me with half-clenched smiles. Molly, a woman with helmet-shaped hair and a pear-shaped frame, was in the office directly to my right. She took me around to introduce me after everyone got settled. As she introduced me, I shifted back and forth, unable to get comfortable. The other employees pursed their lips and gave me sideways glances. Some even *tsk-tsked* in my direction.

It took two weeks of skating around, learning the phone system and the basics of Excel, before I made my first big mistake. I made what I thought was the perfect cup of coffee and placed it on Mr. Copper's desk. He was on the phone. Without looking up, he picked it up, took a sip, and placed it back on his desk. He turned away from his computer and glared at me, biting his lip. "Let me call you right back." He placed the phone on the receiver with slow precision. "What's this?" he asked, gesturing at the cup.

"Your coffee."

"I'm not an idiot. What's *in* it?"

"Oh. Two creams, one sugar."

"It's supposed to be one cream, two sugars."

"I'm so sorry. I'll make you another." I wrapped my hands behind my back to hold my own elbows.

"Don't bother." He picked up the phone. *Shit. He's calling someone to escort me out.* "Molly? Bring me a coffee. Thanks." *Thank God! I'm not fired.* He hung up the phone and looked at me. "I don't like mistakes."

"It won't happen again. I promise."

He shooed me out the door, and I skittered out like a mouse. Outside his office I passed Molly, red-faced and running in with coffee.

After that, things plummeted downward like a rollercoaster hill, complete with that soured stomach feeling. I couldn't get Excel to line up properly when I printed it, and I couldn't get the correct lines to add and multiply like he wanted. I opened several pieces of mail on the wrong end, ripping the letters inside.

I killed the freaking plant.

Even the things I didn't do were my fault somehow. If the mail was late, I got a call. If the phone lines were full and the boss couldn't get through, he'd walk to the spiral staircase and grit his teeth.

I hated the advertising agency, loathed seeing my boss's number pop up on the caller ID. My hands trembled each time I entered the building.

In contrast, my weekends at Fettuccine's were fun. I forgot about how awful I smelled from the garlic and how heavy the headset was, and I enjoyed working with my friends.

Monday through Friday I tiptoed around, doing my best not to burn the coffee, print documents on the wrong paper, or answer calls in two-and-a-half rings instead of two.

On my last day, Mr. Copper called me. "Come to my office."

I rolled my eyes. "Okay."

I scaled the spiral staircase for the last time and entered his office.

"Just buy the damn thing," he seethed into the phone. "Love you, bye."

I stood at the door waiting, timid.

He glanced up at me. "Sit, please." He waved me in absently. I did as I was told and sat on the edge of an oversized leather chair. "That was my wife. She's used to getting what she wants. From the right side of the tracks."

I nodded. *Why is he telling me this?*

"You and I, we're different. Hard workers. From lower class." He handed me a plain white envelope. "It's your last check." He didn't even use a fancy letterhead envelope.

I offered him a thin smile, no teeth.

"I don't think I need to tell you we aren't keeping you on," he said, tilting his head back.

"No, I know. I have another job."

"Good. Keep making good choices. I'm sure you'll find success." His voice was firm and direct.

"Thanks."

"I mean that."

Later that day, with his words hanging in the air, I decided to move back home. "I'm sorry, Chrystal."

"I'll miss you, but I understand. We can load up my truck this weekend," she said.

"Thanks for the help."

"You bet." She turned to walk down the short hallway toward our bedrooms.

"Chrystal?"

"Yeah?" She stopped and spun around.

"Mind if I use your computer? I want to print off a college application."

Freckles

In July of 2002, my almost-twenty-one-year-old brain didn't want to commit to anything except having a good time. I had just moved out of Chrystal's and back in with my parents to save money, but I didn't want to be there with them. I needed time and space to find out who I was.

Jim rarely talked to me, and when he did, we argued. He smelled like car grease from all the hours he spent outside, away from me and Brittany, working on his bikes and cars. We had nothing in common, just two people living under the same roof who sometimes brushed shoulders while passing each other in the kitchen, looking for snacks in the cupboard.

I hadn't dated anyone seriously since Kyle broke up with me and went back to his baby's momma. Not that I wanted to be a stepmom at nineteen, but between my relationships with him and Jim, I believed men were big fat jerks.

I had been going out less and studying more. I added summer classes to my schedule because I didn't want to backpedal into being irresponsible; I had to keep moving forward toward something other than living at home and working shitty jobs.

One night, a friend invited me to his party to celebrate his roommate's recent breakup. His roommate's name was Justin.

I didn't know Justin, but I'd noticed him around before. All I knew was that he was a cute guy who spiked his blond hair and played slap bass. I was a band fan—always going to shows and interviewing bands. At the time, I wrote for *The Glass Eye*, a music zine in Toledo. It wasn't a *real* job; I didn't get paid. But writing was the one thing that put a smile on my face. Since the advertising agency had been a total flop, my new goal was to write for *Rolling Stone*.

Justin's band, Stunnd, had played at a little Irish pub downtown once while I was there with friends. They sounded like Nickelback or maybe Three Doors Down. I had liked watching him play.

I agreed to go to the party, then stewed for hours over what to wear. All my friends had other plans, and I contemplated bailing. No one would have missed me, anyway. But Justin would be there, and even though I was taking that time to figure myself out, maybe I wanted to give dating another chance. I went alone.

At the party, a red light on the end table provided the only light in the otherwise dark living room. I didn't mind the darkness because I thought it would hide my anxiety. Stale smoke had settled, and people situated themselves on couches or cross-legged on the floor. I hugged a few acquaintances.

Someone said, "There's beer in the fridge, Danielle. Help yourself." I did.

I drank faster than normal because I needed to fill the space and calm my nerves. After two beers, I moved closer to Justin and his spiky hair, but didn't speak to him. Instead, I lost myself in conversation with strangers who were less intimidating.

After I was sufficiently buzzed from the beer, Justin brushed my shoulder with his and said, "Excuse me," and, "You're Danielle, right?" My cheeks simmered.

Then he said, "We match because we both have freckles." He leaned toward me and smiled a boyish grin.

"You're funny." I laughed and smiled back.

Pigs in a Blanket

The following month, I said to Petra, Justin's mom, "Thank you for inviting me to dinner tonight. What are you making? It smells good."

"German cabbage rolls," she said while stirring at the stove.

"Pigs in a blanket?" I asked. Petra nodded. I could smell cabbage, meat, and onions. "Yum."

I joined Justin, my new boyfriend, at the small dinner table in the corner of his mom's living room. Petra lived in a clean, modern townhome in the "good" part of Toledo. She had nice cream leather couches, no pets, and a ficus tree with Christmas lights in the middle of the summer. A bowl of fake, glittering fruit sat in the middle of the table: grapes, a pear, and some apples. I touched them and realized the sparkles were thousands of beads. Fancy.

"What do you *do*, Danielle?" Petra called from the galley kitchen. Through the threshold, I watched her poke the rolls in the pot. Her thin yet stoic German frame and short blond hair made me nervous. I tucked stray hairs behind my ears.

Justin and I were a brand-new couple, and I didn't belong there yet.

"I'm in school. And I work two jobs," I said.

She spun to face me, and I couldn't help but compare her to my own mother, who was soft, dark, and kind. They seemed so different. Petra stared at me, and my skin went prickly. "So, you're responsible, then?" She stared directly into my eyes, waiting for an answer. I knew she was testing me, making sure I was an acceptable match for her only son.

༄

In 1986, at five years old, I stood in Grandma's kitchen in the space between the stove, the counter, and the table. Two doors were on the opposite wall: one that led outside, and one that led to the basement, where Grandpa shelved the pickles and tomatoes he canned each year. I never once went down the steps to see what it was like, but I imagined cobwebs and spiders and dark creepy shadows stretching along old cement walls.

The kitchen smelled like pork, beef, onions, cabbage, and Grandpa's stewed tomatoes.

Grandma hovered over the stove wearing her frilly blue vintage apron that had little red apples dotting it. One hand stirred a big metal pot and the other rested on her hip.

On the counter beneath the windowsill, dentures soaked in a clear cup. I squinted, imagining them talking and maybe blowing some bubbles as they flapped in the water.

"Smile for me, Gramma," I said.

She turned from the pot, wire curlers still set in her hair, hand never leaving her hip. Then Grandma smiled wide, curling her lips over her gums and sticking out her tongue. We laughed.

"Whatcha makin'?" I asked her.

"Pigs in a blanket." She winked.

I stood on my toes to see inside the pot. Perfect tubes of wrapped meat bobbed in red juice as she poked and stirred again.

"Yum," I said and whirled to run my finger along the yellow kitchen wall. I traced invisible smiley faces on the paint that was sticky with years of kitchen grease. "My favorite color is yellow."

"Why's that?" she asked, slightly lisp-y from her lack of teeth. She was distracted by a squirrel in the backyard.

"I dunno. I guess 'cause it's the color of the sun. Yellow is a happy color."

"Makes sense." She gave me another toothless smile and shuffled around the kitchen, scraping the linoleum with the bottoms of her slippers.

⌒

In 1995, my freshman year of high school, I walked into Mom's house and dropped my backpack in the middle of the living room floor. I gave each dog a quick rub on the head, then noticed the smell of cooked cabbage, meat, and tomatoes sifting into my nose. I found Mom stirring a pot at the stove.

"What smells so good? I'm starving."

"Pigs in a blanket. Don't you eat at school? It's not even four o'clock yet."

I kissed Mom on the cheek. "I had a bagel and Skittles at lunch." I said as I flopped down on a barstool, exhausted from school. I glanced around the kitchen. That year, Mom had wallpapered a border around the top of the kitchen that was patterned with a flying flock of ducks wearing floppy hats. A wooden duck holding a sign that said "Welcome" hung on the wall next to the fridge. I think she bought it at a craft show. This was around the same time everyone had cement geese on their front porches wearing things like raincoats and bikinis, depending on the weather. Mom liked to redecorate often, so I knew the duck phase wouldn't last.

I traced my index finger along the grout of the tile counters Jim poured with his own hands. "But it won't have Grandpa's tomatoes."

"It'll be close enough. Wanna eat at the dining table today?" she asked.

"Sure." Eating at the table was a rare occurrence in our house. Jim always sat in front of the television. Mom, Brittany, and I ate in the kitchen.

"Can you wipe it down for me?" Mom asked.

"Sure." I moved the antique doily from the center of the table and wiped away the dust with a wet rag. Bits of dog hair and car grease collected on the tips of my fingers, so I washed them before gathering forks, knives, and paper towels.

Tears burned my eyes when I glanced at the photo of my grandparents, still holding hands in their sixties. It sat on the antique bureau, in the same place it had been since before my grandpa and grandma each passed away. "I miss Grandma and Grandpa," I said to Mom.

"Me too." Mom gave me a half-smile from the other side of the pass-through window connecting the kitchen to the dining room.

～

In 2002, Petra put the bowl of cabbage rolls in front of me. They were similar in shape, but thin brown gravy covered my pigs in a blanket instead of stewed tomatoes.

"Have you ever had this before?" Petra asked and sat beside me. She picked up her fork and knife then stared, waiting for me to take the first bite.

"I have. But . . . it was a little different," I said. The nutmeg wafted up to my nose, and I decided to give them a try. I cleared my throat, worried about accidentally scraping the bowl with my fork or placing my knife in the wrong place.

After a few sharp breaths to steady my nerves, I cut into my pig, and the consistency was nearly identical. The cabbage unraveled, exposing the mixture of meat and breadcrumbs. Grandma used rice to hold the meat together, but it was similar. I jabbed a bit of everything onto my fork. When I ate it, notes of thyme and beef stock mixed with the onions and meat. It couldn't replace my grandma's recipe, but it could hold its own special place in my heart.

⤺

In 1986, I said, "And, Gramma?"

"What's that, baby girl?"

"My favorite food is pigs in a blanket."

"Mine too." Grandma winked and pulled her favorite delicate pink and green bowls from the cupboard.

Dressed in White

On July 15, 2005, the night before my wedding, I sat on my parents' kitchen floor, painting my toenails while sipping Bud Lights with my sister. Hardly glamorous. Instead of crisp Egyptian cotton bedding on a king-sized pillow-top mattress, I sauntered to my childhood bedroom before ten o'clock.

While lying in my old twin bed, I looked at the art on the walls. Nothing had changed. The bedtime prayer hung next to the door where Jim hammered the nail after he finished the home's addition, and the plaster figurines Mom painted sat on the dresser. There was one of me in God's palm, another in a bright green dress, and another of a girl with pigtails holding a stuffed bunny. I never paid much attention to them before, but these things had always been there to remind me that Mom and Jim loved me.

Justin loved me too.

Our relationship moved quickly, according to some of our friends. After dating for only three months, we'd moved into an apartment together. But the timing had felt right to us. His lease was up, and I had turned twenty-one while still living back at home with my parents. He became more than my boyfriend. He became my best friend. Decisions were easy to make when we worked together as a team. I'd never had something like that before.

Like Mom and Don had been, we were broke. Justin worked security for the apartment we lived in, and I managed a record store while writing for *The Glass Eye*. And like Mom and Don, we didn't date long before getting engaged. After only two years of dating, he proposed at our favorite Italian restaurant with reddened, tear-filled eyes. Unlike Mom and Don, I knew our relationship was one that would last.

I wasn't nervous about getting married. Not at all. I couldn't wait to get married, but I didn't want it all to end: the planning, the doting, the dress, and the cake-shopping. Justin and I breathed nothing but the sweet smells of wedding plans for a year. I didn't want to go back to regular old air.

In the morning, Brittany, Kate, and I giggled all the way to the salon. Once there, curls, hairspray, and seventy-two bobby pins wrangled my hair into the updo I picked.

"Put in the veil like this," my stylist said to Brittany.

"I can do that," she promised with a smile.

Later that day, at the church, I slipped into the twelve layers of tulle, clasped the jewelry, and adjusted the garter belt. Mom buttoned the dress. It was the strapless one I had to have, with tiny sequins sewn into the shape of flowers across the front and down the length, scattered along the six-foot train, which Justin's mom had added Swarovski crystals to for extra sparkle.

My sister had trouble getting the veil to stay in because of all the bobby pins. She added more pins to hold it steady. "It will be fine," I said as someone knocked on the door. "Come in," I called.

Jim opened the door, looking dapper in his silver and black tuxedo. "It's time," he said. I nodded.

I walked up the stairs outside my dressing room and entered the sanctuary through the main church doors. My elementary music teacher began playing Pachelbel's "Canon in D Major" on the organ. That was my cue to walk down the aisle. Family and friends sat in polished wooden pews to my left and right, and candles at the altar filled the room with a soft, flowery smell. In front of me stood the pastor at the altar, offering me an encouraging grin. Beside the pastor was Justin in the tuxedo we'd chosen together. Our eyes connected and air caught in my throat. His cheeks were flushed and his eyes were wet, and it looked as though he was crying happy tears.

On either side of Justin and the pastor stood the bridal party. Our best friends; our family. I hoped those people would be the people we could count on throughout any tough time we endured. With each step toward them, my heels sank into the plush green carpet, and I was thankful I had Jim's arm keeping me upright.

I hadn't even sent Don an invitation. I knew he wouldn't come. But I reserved a seat in the front row for Grandma and Grandpa, both in heaven.

Jim handed me off to Justin and joked, "Good luck with this one," in a whisper. Justin stifled a smile. I wanted to punch them both. Instead, I clamped my arms down at my sides to prevent my dress from slipping too much.

As I read my vows, I reminded myself what kind of marriage I expected to have with Justin. It wouldn't be anything like the relationship between Don and my mom, but maybe it would be something like what Jim and Mom had together. More than anything, I wanted to spend the rest of my life with my best friend, a person who could always make me laugh.

After I said, "I do," I looked up into Justin's green eyes and I remembered the joke he made about our freckles years ago. We kissed, and the pastor announced us as husband and wife.

Detroit Has a Heartbeat

When I moved to Detroit with Justin after our wedding and his acceptance to the University of Detroit Law School, my parents were afraid of what they thought they knew about the city. They mentioned drugs, murders, and gangs. But those things didn't make Detroit what it was.

I tried to convince them to look harder, dig deeper, and really inhale the city. If they did, they would've found a moment to enjoy the beauty. They would've seen what makes Detroit special.

Driving up 95 North to my sunny loft on Adams, Tiger Stadium and the Michigan Central Station loomed, both eerie skeletons full of deterioration. But they belonged there as much as the skyscrapers. The skyline was a mix of ornate pre-war facades and newer structures with sharp angles made of steel and glass. All of these buildings breathed the wind that blew up Grand Central Boulevard into downtown. In. Out. Their frames expanding, contracting.

The night the Tigers baseball team won the American League Championship in 2006, I ran down Woodward chanting for Magglio Ordoniez along with thousands of other people. As I shared high fives with strangers in cars and on the sidewalks under the chill of the October moon, I knew Detroit had a rock-solid heartbeat.

It pounded through my chest like a beat-up sledgehammer, dirty and noisy but powerful and captivating. Detroit's energy was palpable and irresistible—invisible, but always touching my fingertips like a current running through electrical wires. It was tangible, as solid as the giant Joe Lewis Fist statue, a gift to Detroit from *Sports Illustrated Magazine*.

When I danced at Detroit's electronic music festival, Movement, the vibration of Detroit's heart resonated along the river in Hart Plaza. It thumped with the music, swelled with the air, and dripped with the sweat of thousands of people dressed in wild colors.

At Lafayette Coney Island, arguably the best place in the country for a late-night hot dog, it was the secret ingredient in the chili. The employees there worked together like a well-oiled machine, making hot dog masterpieces to satisfy hungry bellies all night long.

I took one look at the casino lights and saw it there, bright as day. I heard it in the *ca-ching* of the slot machines, and it revved in the rushing roll of the roulette ball.

The auto industry had catalyzed the growth of Detroit years before. It was about as American as it gets, built by blue-collar families. At one time, people flocked to Detroit for the promise of a house with the white picket fence and a patch of driveway for their American-made automobile. It was the city of the coveted dream. People were ready to put in the hard work, because they believed in what Detroit *could* be.

The spirit of those American dream chasers lives on, lingering in the concrete poured to construct Woodward Avenue, in the steel beams supporting the iconic GM Renaissance Center, and even in the crowd cheering when the pigskin is caught by a Lion in the end zone. The pride they carried still rushes with the river, lapping up against Belle Isle Beach.

Then, now, always: the Motor City has a pulse.

Shot Girl

When we first moved to Detroit, we'd walk to this dirty pub called Danny's for cheap drinks with Justin's law school friends and their girlfriends on the weekends. A mostly empty bar ran the length of the front room. It had three pool tables and a unisex bathroom that didn't lock. The back room was a small square with red lights and a cement floor.

The girls and I spent our time dancing on top of the bar to songs like "Gold Digger" and "Don't Cha," drinking free neon pink shots. On Friday and Saturday nights, we walked home sloshy and sloppy. Some weekends Brittany would come up from Toledo to get away from Mom and Jim. I'd dress her up like a life-sized doll and get her tipsy before we went out. It was fun until the money ran low.

When the cost of new clothes for the bar got too high, I told the owner, Danny, that I needed a job. Justin didn't work because law school was too demanding, and I was selling refurbished cell phones for commission at a shady store near Wayne State University. It wasn't enough to pay the rent on our five-hundred-square-foot apartment, much less for nice things and beer.

He eyed me for a moment. "Ever bartend?"

I shook my head and said, "I work hard, though."

He shrugged. "Fine. You can start tomorrow."

"Great!" I clasped my hands together and hopped. Just like that, I was the bar's newest shot girl.

The following night, I traded my bar dancing heels for responsible flats and arrived at Danny's before ten. I had never seen it so empty. Danny's was a place for people to go when other bars closed. There, they could continue drinking well past Michigan's law of two a.m. The crowd stumbled in late and rowdy.

Danny taught me to pour a simple shot without spilling. "Count to four for a single and eight for a double." And how to carry a tray through a crowd of people. "Rest the tray on your fingers while you're walking."

I practiced pouring with a bottle of water and walked around the empty bar with a tray and a single shot glass on top. "Easy enough."

"Be nice to the customers. Flirt with them, even," he instructed. "Any tips you make are yours to keep."

I gulped down my pride. The thought of flirting with customers for tips made my skin crawl, but we really needed the cash. I decided to meet him somewhere in the middle and smile coyly. Nothing more.

"And if they offer you a shot, take it. But don't drink it. Bring it back to the bar and put it there." He motioned to a thin shelf on the back wall.

Only a few customers meandered into the back bar before midnight, but after that, people filed in fast. I zigzagged back and forth between dancers as Beyoncé and Christina Aguilera filled the air with danceable beats. The bass hit so hard it rattled my teeth.

Though I offered to grab customers their next drink, most people went straight to Danny. He was the friendly face of the bar. I was a stranger with an empty tray taking orders.

"Nobody wants anything from me," I said to Danny around one a.m.

"Take these." He handed me a tray of the coveted neon pink shots.

I swallowed hard, not sure I'd be able to keep the liquor in the shot glasses. I took the tray anyway, holding it across the top of my hand like he showed me, and moved through the crowd. "I've got this," I said to myself.

The shots disappeared before I made it to the end of the room, and a pile of bills sat on my tray in their place. I walked back to the bar, proud and ready for a refill.

Danny took the cash, and I stuffed the tips in my back pocket.

He handed me another tray. "Great job."

"Thanks!" I said and made my next round.

Just after two a.m., a loud boom near the bar's wall of windows startled me into a yelp. One gunshot. And then another and another—three booms, interrupted by screams and dropped drinks. The music stopped.

"What the—" a large man beside me said. My eyes flitted to him, then the bar, confused. Were the shots inside? Outside? I couldn't tell.

Danny grabbed me by my shoulder and yanked me behind the bar. "Stay down. Don't move."

I listened and knelt down, no longer able to see the commotion in the room. The sounds of shuffling feet, muffled sobs, and distressed voices filled my ears. I could only imagine what the drunk customers were doing on the other side of my barricade. A puddle of spilled liquor drenched my knees. The smell of stale beer and soda syrup made me gag, so I covered my mouth with my hand and stared at the shelf in front of me filled with paper towels and cleaning supplies. It was such a mess. Everything was just crammed in there, angled and wedged like a game of cleaning supply Tetris. I focused on that so I wouldn't have to think of anything else.

"I'll kill a motherfucker," said one voice.

"I've got kids. Oh God, my kids," another cried.

"Everyone please be quiet and stay calm," Danny said.

The bouncer paged him on the walkie-talkie. "Danny?"

I gazed up to see Danny running to grab the walkie from the shelf behind me. "What's going on out there?" he asked his bouncer.

"We've locked the doors. There's a man waving a gun around outside. Looks drunk. Police are trying to detain him."

Danny bent down. "You should call your husband."

My heart thrashed against my ribs. I looked around in the red light for my bag. It was within reach, so I plucked it from the shelf and dug around to find my flip phone. My hands shook uncontrollably as I dialed Justin's number. The phone rang just once.

"Hello?" Justin answered.

"Babe. I'm okay, really I'm okay, but someone has a gun outside Danny's. He fired a bunch of shots. I'm scared," I whispered.

"Are you serious?" he asked.

"I wouldn't joke about this." I said.

"Shit. Okay. I'll stay on the phone with you. Try to stay calm."

"I'll try."

I didn't even want to breathe. I kept thinking about the possibility of the man firing another shot toward the bar. *What if it goes right through the window and injures someone? What if it's me? What if I never see the outside of this bar again? What if the last thing I see is this stupid pile of paper towels shoved onto a shelf?*

Danny's walkie-talkie beeped. "Police have detained him. They say it's safe to leave now." Danny looked at me and patted my shoulder.

"Justin? It's over. Come get me." No wad of ones was worth a bullet. I would rather be broke than be a shot girl ever again.

"On my way."

I hung up and turned to Danny. "Danny, I don't know if I can—"

"It's okay, kid. I understand." He winked at me. "See you and Justin next week for a drink?"

"Maybe." I shrugged. We both knew he wouldn't.

When Everything Changed

Two months into living in Detroit, after getting our only car stolen at my job selling refurbished phones and feeling a bit like stepped-on shit, I finally caught a break. I got a good job working at a health insurance agency. My duties were comprised of taking numbers from a sheet of paper and typing them onto a screen: ID numbers, birthdays, ages, transaction types, and plan codes. If it sounds boring, that's because it was. But at twenty-three, it was the most responsible thing I'd ever done.

At work, I wore floaty dresses and boot-cut dress pants from Express, cute kitten heels, and a badge that said I *belonged* there. Considering I had belonged nowhere except the poor kid's club and maybe my job buttering breadsticks as a teenager, I'd say things were on the upswing.

Justin and I had a nice loft downtown. We had vintage windows on old chain-and-pull systems, parquet wood floors, and a little machine that washed and dried clothes. Never mind the fact that it took two hours to dry our clothes, and sometimes they reeked of burnt cotton when they were done. We had the machine, and that's more than I can say for any other time before in my life.

If we had lived in any other big city, my husband and I wouldn't have been able to afford it. But in Detroit, we could. Barely.

With my new job to pay for it, on the weekends we partied at Bleu, an electronic music nightclub. We drank ten-dollar Jäger bombs until two in the morning, sometimes three nights a week. Going to nightclubs made me feel important. The alcohol softened my anxiety and encouraged me to smile for real. Dancing with my friends was a way to escape.

Justin and I wore new shoes and jeans, paid for by my job and his student loan living expense money, and we fit nicely into this new role of a young married couple living in the city.

We had friends we met through a website called Detroit Club Scene. There were at least twenty of us. To us, young adulthood was all about the fun. No real responsibilities. No kids. No mortgage. No sickness.

Life was great.

On a normal workday in December 2008, two years into my job and fancy life, while typing up my third or fourth stack of paperwork for the day and blaring Fall Out Boy through my headphones, my pink flip phone shimmied across my desk. I checked the caller ID.

Mom? Living an hour away from her added tension to our relationship, but we handled it okay. We talked at least once or twice a week, and she'd even been up to visit me, but only once because Detroit still scared her. But she never called me at work. She just didn't. I jumped up with my phone and jogged outside to the hallway to call her back. Something didn't feel right. I dialed her number, and she answered right away.

"Hey, Mom what's up?" I tapped my foot on the carpeted floor.

"Pumpkin," she said.

Pumpkin was the nickname she used when she needed to be extra loving. It was the name that reminded me of sick days home from school, or the times we had to sacrifice things for food on the table. It reminded me of when I burned my hands on the kerosene heater and when each grandparent died.

"What's wrong?" I asked her. I stopped tapping and started pacing.

I heard her take a drawn-out drag from her cigarette. I almost saw the exhale as it hit the receiver on her end. I knew she had her hand pressed to her forehead. Maybe Jim had lost his job again, and they would have another disappointing Christmas. Maybe my sister had started dating another guy my parents didn't approve of.

"Danielle, I went to the doctor today. I had a colonoscopy done a few days ago. Routine, but they found something," she said. My heart found its way up to my throat.

"What, Mom? What did they find?" I think I may have been yelling. I licked my lips and then bit my tongue while she finished.

"I-I . . . Oh, Danielle, they found a mass. They tested it, hoping it was benign, but it isn't."

I didn't understand why she was being so damn vague.

"What does that even mean? I don't understand what you're saying."

"It means I'm sick. Very sick," she sighed.

"So get better." It was the obvious answer.

"Danielle, I have cancer."

And just like that, my world, which had finally been looking up, fell over like a house of cards. The job, the loft, the stupid laundry machine. None of it mattered anymore.

The word "cancer" and all of its ugliness kept snaking its way back and forth in my brain. It got louder and louder, and Mom's voice traveled farther away from me, fading. I fell to my knees.

I remember nothing else until I walked in the door to my empty apartment.

"Hello?" I called out. Justin was at school. I'd hoped that somehow he would be home. I didn't want to be alone, but there I was.

At the sight of my bed, I crawled in and heaved tears and curse words into my pillow. Growing up sucked.

When Justin came home from class—early because I guess someone at work must've called to let him know—he found me this way. An incoherent, red-faced mess. He pulled me into his arms and promised me that everything would be fine. He told me he was going to take me to see Mom so I could see she was still okay, that she wasn't disappearing like a mirage. I loved him even more after that moment.

Toledo is a one hour drive from Detroit. It's a straight shot south on I-75 to get there. Factories, cornfields, and a nuclear power plant dragged by my line of sight. Gray clouds in the sky muted the dead grass. Everything was so drab. My state of mind changed the world outside my head, or maybe I was only starting to see the world for what it really was.

When we finally pulled into her driveway on Custer Drive, I saw Mom there, sitting on the porch, smoking her cigarettes, and drinking her coffee. Everything about her on the outside was exactly the same. Same skin, same smile, same eyes and hair. It reassured me that she was still okay. I jumped out of the car to meet her at the steps. Hugging her was the best, most reassuring moment I'd ever experienced. Her Rave hairspray and patchouli perfume filled my nose. Her soft shoulders and arms still tightened around me the same.

"I'm so glad you came," she said to me.

"Me too."

I decided to ignore her cancer and pretend that everything was exactly the same as it used to be. And she decided not to bring it up to me much. But we both knew the truth. Nothing would ever really be the same.

Trigger

A few months after Mom found out she had cancer, we had finally found some normalcy again. Mom started a twice-monthly chemotherapy routine, Justin had school and the bar exam to study for, and I had work.

Detroit had become our home. We had friends, people who were just like us: they didn't come with money-lined pockets, they had roughened fingers from working blue-collar jobs, and they liked to party on the weekends after long weeks of working overtime. I never wanted to be anywhere else. Those were my people. Detroit was my city.

But, unfortunately, the auto industry was collapsing around us, and since Detroit's economy had been built on the automobile, Detroit was crumbling too, along with my heart.

One rainy Sunday, Justin and I loaded up our car with groceries for the week. We couldn't get groceries in downtown Detroit because big chains refused to put stores there. Not enough rich white people lived in my neighborhood. The smaller stores near Wayne State University were overpriced with near-rotten produce and questionably colored meats. Instead, we drove to Dearborn every week, a twenty-minute ride, for food. I always wondered about the people living in the city who couldn't afford a car or insurance bill, the ones who relied on the bus to get them back and forth. They were forgotten, forced to buy whatever they could get within a walkable or bus ride's distance.

"Are you studying today?" I asked Justin.

"Not today. Let's watch a movie." He was close to being done with law school, and with his graduation so tangible, he was burnt out on reviewing case law.

We drove past the casino with the top floor restaurant where we had eaten perfectly cooked, medium rare steaks with wild mushrooms for our second anniversary. Inside the restaurant, a wine shelf rotated behind a glass wall that stretched all the way up to the thirty-foot ceilings. The best views of Detroit's skyline I'd ever seen were through their massive windows. We were fortunate to be able to afford dinner there.

I smiled at Justin and glanced forward as he turned the car onto our street. Three teenagers dressed in Tiger blue—a normal-looking group of kids—walked on the sidewalk next to my side of the car. We drove our coupe up behind them and stopped at the red light, just as they entered the street to cross in front of our car. I was thinking about the week ahead and all the overtime I'd be working when they turned to look in our direction.

"Get the fuck out of my D!" one of them shouted and startled me.

"My, God. Danielle, he's got a gun," Justin said. My eyes darted up. His gun, small and silver, was pointed right at my face.

"Shit." My heart pounded in my ears. I grabbed my husband's arm, digging my nails into his bicep. With my other hand, I fidgeted with the seatbelt. I twisted the thick gray fabric, wishing it were made of something stronger. The light turned green, but Justin had to wait for them to finish crossing the street.

I looked the kid with a gun straight in his darkened and narrowed eyes.

His brows distorted and nostrils flared. My breath turned to sludge inside my throat.

People say your life flashes before your eyes in situations like that. Not me. Time stopped, and I sat there, frozen, waiting for him to end our lives with a bullet.

"I said get the fuck out of my city!" he repeated.

Acid burned the back of my throat. My heart quickened as Justin finally floored the gas, thrusting my shoulders into my seat. I knew it would be so easy for this kid to pull the trigger, to take his anger out on us. What would his choice matter in the moment? Everything to him, everything to us.

Detroit hadn't been the same since the riots of 1967 and the white flight that followed. It was a time for significant downhill change for the city, filled with violence and death. Whites against blacks; cops against civilians. White residents fled by the thousands to the suburbs. When they moved, they took prosperity and left a lasting footprint of decay seen even today. There is a racial divide so deep that time hasn't been able to repair it. Transplants (like myself) don't get it at first, but the people born and raised in Detroit have hot blood coursing through their veins, fifty years later.

But he didn't pull the trigger.

Leaving Detroit[5]

"See you soon," I said to my husband after he kissed me goodbye in Detroit. He left for New York to establish his career and our new lives together. I stayed in our apartment to pack for thirty days.

It was the white flight all over, only I was the white, and it was my flight. Detroit had been mostly good to us for three years, and there I was running off when things got tough.

I stared down at my hands, wondering what to do first. Settling on clothes, I went through my closet, folding and stuffing shirts in cardboard boxes. Long sleeves first, because it was almost summer. I packed jeans and dresses on their hangers. It would make unpacking in our new home easier. I left out the sweatshirt with the Old English style letter "D" because I thought I might need it at night when the cool breeze bit from the Detroit River. I sighed.

In the kitchen, I wrapped glasses in grocery bags because I couldn't afford bubble wrap or newspaper. I didn't have many pots or pans, just a few hand-me-downs from Mom. The thought of keeping one out crossed my mind. But I decided to live on sandwiches, salads, and cereal. It was only a month, after all. I packed them away and taped the box shut.

I left the things I wouldn't have room for in my new city slumped next to the trash chute: old artwork and chairs from Ikea that wouldn't fit in the truck, the ripped Nelly Furtado hoodie that held memories of late nights and laughter in its pocket, the s-shaped shelf that once displayed photos of friends.

Each day after work, I walked my dog, Roxy, around Comerica Park, trying to recall the way home runs echoed off my favorite players' bats. I

---

5 A version of this essay was previously published in *Beach Reads: Adrift.*

remembered the chants for Magglio, Verlander's no-hitter, and Zumia's wicked fastball. I asked myself if watching the Yankees would give me the same joy. Would I forget how much I loved nestling into the crowd for a Saturday night game?

I stopped in front of the gate to see the green field. I closed my eyes and imagined the taste of a Hebrew National hot dog with just mustard, sweat pooling on my back before the August sun would drop behind the top of the stadium. Would the sunsets look different in Brooklyn? Would the sky change from blue to pink and crimson before settling in below the trees? Would the buildings be too tall to see the beauty? Would my neighborhood even have trees to look at, to breathe in autumn, to catch snow in winter, and to bloom in the spring?

Before the move, I invited my friends over one last time. The ones who had been there for the parties, for the fun, but also for the real moments: Anna, whose hair I'd saved from a candle at the first Detroit party I went to; Sam, the sweet blond with an infectious laugh; and Matilda, an artist from next door. We danced. We sang. We reminisced about the late-night parties in my apartment.

"No one will ever replace you guys. You are literally the best." A heaviness filled my chest as I looked them in the eyes and promised them I would never let go, even with hundreds of miles stretching between my palms and theirs. They promised the same.

When Justin came home thirty days later, I kissed him and hugged him, allowing his strong arms to secure me. I breathed in his heady cologne.

I reminded myself why we were going: his career, our future together. Detroit was crumbling around us; the auto industry had collapsed again. My job had offered me a voluntary severance, but others weren't so lucky. If we stayed, the s-shaped shelf and happy faces in those photos would fall to dust with this city. I had to leave and salvage what was left.

I watched all my things get loaded into the truck: blue leather couch, old dresser, favorite vintage lamp. One by one they left my home. There were things that couldn't fit: the skyline, my favorite bar, my friends, my heart. Those were the things we had to leave behind.

I said goodbye to what was left: the empty apartment space, the parquet wood floors, the echo off the avocado-green walls, the memories of home.

I told myself it was okay to cry.

Living in Bushwick

I loved New York: the screeching subways, the sidewalk Mariachi band members wearing shoes made of real alligators, the shopping in SoHo, the twenty-dollar drinks at the hole-in-the-wall pubs, and the high-paying jobs by midwestern standards—even my new job as a paralegal. The good, the great, and the wild; I loved it all.

But it wasn't home.

Our first place in New York was a railroad-style apartment, which meant each room opened into the next—long and narrow. The apartment had end-to-end original pine floors, exposed brick, and twenty-foot ceilings, and it sat on such a bad slant that round things often rolled from one end of the kitchen to the other. The tile in the bathroom had little pink roses on it and was the tackiest feature of our apartment at first glance. There were only four small kitchen cabinets we had to cram our things into. I missed my open Detroit loft.

Bushwick, where we lived, was a Hispanic area that had been renamed East Williamsburg to gentrify it and attract more young white people. I liked Bushwick better. The name change was meant to mimic the hipster-friendly Williamsburg, where posh restaurants shared walls with dive bars and boutique clothing stores, nestled under the famous blue Williamsburg Bridge. But my neighborhood wasn't anything like Williamsburg, and for that I was happy.

We bought our vegetables and fruits from cash-only stands on the side of the street. We walked Roxy through Maria Hernandez Park, where guys played handball and girls watched from outside the court, laughing and chatting. Upbeat Hispanic music blared from boom boxes. These things I loved most about Bushwick: the culture and the simple fun outside the big, ferocious city. Still, I missed the guys playing saxophone on the corner in

Greektown, the food in Mexicantown (which was the best, most authentic Mexican food I'd ever had), and most of all, I missed my friends.

A thin, elderly man with leathery brown skin who often perched himself on the stoop next to ours became my first New York buddy. He always smelled like tequila and cigarettes. Originally from Puerto Rico, he vowed to teach me Spanish.

"Say '*hola*.'"

"Oh-la?"

"Spanish for hello." He nodded and pulled a Marlboro Red from his linen shirt pocket.

"Hola!" I said and waved.

He struck a match against the brick building and lit his cigarette, taking a long, slow drag. "*Muy bien*," he said through a cloud of smoke.

He told me stories about Bushwick. "They used to call this street Vietnam," he said. "Garbage cans with fires in the middle of the street. Drugs. Killings. *Muy mal*."

"Moo-ey mal?" I asked.

"Very bad."

"I see." I tried to imagine the streets of my new neighborhood on fire, but I couldn't. Instead, I saw a stream of people walking by. Some on their way to work, others out shopping or on their way to the bodega; hard-working, middle-class folks trying to make it in the most expensive city in the country. Dreams can come true in New York if your skin is thick enough. "Why'd you stay?" I asked.

He shrugged and squinted his eyes toward the park. "It's *mi hogar*."

The Biggest Decision

In the beginning, going out was our favorite part of New York. We considered it essential for a good work-life balance. If we had to work long hours at the firm—Justin as a newly minted lawyer and me as his paralegal sidekick—we also had to get drunk afterward to forget the thousands of dollars I'd wired to the wrong bank that day or the contract he'd forgotten to get signed.

On our first Fourth of July in New York, Justin and I climbed the rickety half-broken ladder that led to our apartment building's roof. We braved it, armed with a six-pack of cheap beer, to watch five barges' worth of fireworks on the Hudson River from the top of the world.

We had found several shoebox-sized places to grab a PBR from in Williamsburg, just a couple stops away on the L train. Everyone seemed so hip there with their flannel shirts and plastic-framed glasses. For being so close to Bushwick, it felt worlds apart.

Sometimes we would get adventurous and head out to the city to indulge in bigger clubs. A yellow cab would take us over the Williamsburg Bridge. In the city, lights twinkled so bright it felt like daytime. We tried Pacha and Cielo, both decorated iconic New York nightclubs, but they were too commercial for my taste. Our favorite was the Sullivan Room, nicknamed Sully, which had stone walls and cozy seating along the small perimeter. The electronic music would pound through our chests and make our ears ring by the end of the night.

But getting hammered weekend after weekend in the big city lost its sparkle fast.

"I want a baby," I said to Justin, after a long swig of my beer, four months after moving to Brooklyn. We were sitting on our fire escape, which we had converted to a makeshift patio with milk crates. If we looked left or right, we could see more iron fire escapes with plants, and if we looked forward, we could see the neighbor's collection of backyard junk: car parts, garbage, and weeds. The weather in late August seemed thicker and stickier than I remembered in Detroit. I wiped a dribble of sweat from my neck, beneath my ponytail.

"You what?" He had heard me, but he hadn't *heard* me.

"I. Want. A. Bay. Bee," I repeated.

Justin smiled and laughed. "We can't even keep a plant alive, and we're lucky the dog is so self-sustaining." He stretched out his long legs toward the iron fire escape rails.

"I'm ready."

"I don't know. We have no money saved." He sipped his beer and stared toward the blistering August sun.

"We'll never be financially ready." I moved closer to him, so my shoulder pressed against his.

"You're ready to stop going out, stop spending money, and act like a grown-up?"

"Yep." My stomach fluttered.

"Okay, I guess," he said and shrugged. But then he offered a silly grin.

"Okay," I said. "So why don't we stop trying to *not* have a baby and see what happens?"

"Are you sure you want to do this?" he asked.

"I'm sure."

Back inside, I tossed my last week of pills in the trash.

On October fourth, we were sitting on that same fire escape, drinking a fruity wheat beer and enjoying the crisp fall air that had fallen over Brooklyn.

"My boobs hurt," I told Justin as I pressed on my chest. It felt swollen.

"Yeah?" He laughed. "That's nice."

"No, I mean like *hurt*. Something's not right. I don't feel right."

"Did you take a pregnancy test?"

"Not yet. I don't have one yet. Do you think I should take one?" I could feel my heart race. I tapped my foot against the grated floor.

"Stop drinking," Justin ordered, as he disappeared inside our kitchen window. "Come on. We're getting a test."

"Coming!" I shouted and shimmied back inside.

Ten minutes later, I was back in our kitchen, pacing in front of the bathroom door with the pregnancy test box in my white-knuckled hand.

"I'm not pregnant, I know I'm not." But I couldn't convince myself. I thought, if I am, did I harm my baby with beer and cigarettes? Nervous heat radiated from my face.

"Take the test." Justin leaned against the refrigerator. "Get it over with."

"But I don't have to go right now." The warmth on my cheeks intensified.

"Just try."

I rolled my eyes, walked into the bathroom, and closed the door. I opened the box and unfolded the instructions.

Remove cap from absorbent side of urine stick.

I ripped the cellophane and tossed it into the trash with the box. I pulled the cap off.

Place absorbent side of urine stick in urine for five seconds.

I pulled down my jeans, which felt snugger than usual, and sat on the cold seat, waiting with my hand between my legs, holding onto the pee stick. I could hear my heartbeat in my ears. Finally, a trickle came. I sighed and reread the rest of the instructions.

After sampling, keep absorbent tip pointing downward. Never point absorbent tip upward.

I put the stick on the counter with a bit of toilet paper wedged beneath it and watched the little window on its side.

Wait two minutes.

I thought about baby names, raising a child in a one-bedroom apartment with four cabinets, cockroaches, and the Saturday night impromptu parades down Knickerbocker Avenue.

I didn't notice I'd been holding my breath until I exhaled as the little blue lines appeared on the white stick. In the commercials, people always seemed to know what to say. They had a little speech, some expression of joy or hope. All I could come up with was: "Oh my God, Justin."

"What?" he asked from outside the closed bathroom.

I opened the door to find him stocking the fridge with the beer we had picked up "just in case" I could drink it.

"I'm pregnant," I said. A can escaped Justin's hands and rolled across the kitchen's slanted floor.

Brooklyn Shuffle

We shuffled to and from work in an hour-long car ride, from Brooklyn to Long Island and back. Work shifts stretched past ten hours, and our boss, Alex, was a red-faced screamer. But our coworkers were kind and funny, the truest New Yorkers I'd ever met. Ann (my favorite) was a middle-aged Jewish lady with a bob haircut and an affinity for Dunkin Donuts coffee. Timothy was a short Italian with a quick wit and poorly knotted ties. Lee was a hard-working, super-fast-moving second-year attorney who helped Justin and I navigate the rushing waters of rapid New York real estate closings.

My job was mostly simple: cut checks according to the HUD statements and mail them off to the right places. Justin closed the deals, the last line of defense in making the transactions happen. Our boss often sent him to places anywhere from the Bronx to Staten Island to close loans in the hours after the law firm closed for the day. I tagged along.

Once, we attended a closing on an unseasonably sweltering fall night. The house had no air conditioning. They had covered the dining table and chairs in plastic. When I sat, my legs stuck to the top of the seat like suction cups. An industrial-sized fan faced the table to keep us cool, but the wind created by this monster was fierce. I held down stacks of paper like a human paperweight. Justin shouted document descriptions over the roaring fan blades and the rustling of paper, while his tie whipped around. I was amazed by his ability to keep a straight face.

Another time, our boss sent us from the law office in Long Island all the way to the very end of Staten Island for a closing. The documents came in late from the bank, and we ended up inching along in rush hour traffic, making us almost four hours late to the closing. We closed the refinance at eleven at night, with a slew of angry Italians staring at us.

During this time, our apartment in Bushwick had a growing mouse problem. I hadn't noticed them in May, when we first moved in. But by fall, they were leaving poop trails on my stove, nibbling through wrappers of oatmeal, and chewing holes in the bottom of the dog food bag each night.

Monday through Friday, we woke up at six in the morning, arrived at work by nine, worked in the office until six in the evening, did at least one closing after work, and got home by ten o'clock at night, if luck and traffic were on our side, only for rodent evidence to greet us at the door. Not much of the New York life I'd expected.

One Friday night in late October, I told a new acquaintance about our mice at a rooftop party in Williamsburg. She had bleached hair and a nose ring, and she told me her name was Alice from the Wonderland.

"Oh, that's nothing," she said. "I walked into the kitchen last night and a city rat stared back at me."

Even though she was higher than a kite at Coney Island, I believed her. New York City rats are the size of cats. They eat very well. I figured I shouldn't be so upset about our mouse situation, because things could be worse. After all, our landlord set bait and stuffed steel wool into cracks. That was something.

But day by day, the mice made themselves more welcome. They wiggled under the lid of a plastic tub I bought to secure our food and left little poop nuggets everywhere. They shuffled around the house in the open while we watched *Top Chef* as though we had a legitimate kitchen to cook in. We chased them with a broom to get them to go back inside the walls, and Roxy barked at us. She thought they were her friends. They kept her company while we worked all day in Long Island.

Then one particularly icy Friday in the beginning of November, I reached my limit. We came home to find that the mice had chewed holes through the drywall around the electrical outlets. Our landlord had stuffed steel wool into all the cracks he thought they may be coming through, so the mice constructed themselves new doors. The apartment wasn't ours anymore. It was theirs.

Plus, the heat was off.

Justin called Ali, our landlord, and asked him to come over. Justin showed him the holes in the walls, Ali felt the cold air, and I hid under the winter blankets on our bed.

Justin and Ali closed their talk with a hostile screaming match in the hallway. I could hear every word of it through the paper-thin walls. Thankfully, Ali caved and allowed us to break our lease early, but only after several cuss words.

We convinced Ali to give us back our deposit, despite breaking the lease. I played the pregnancy card, needing a clean, safe place to raise our child. Ali was a father, so he got it. We had to shuffle the money from one bank to another, from Ali's to ours to the real estate agent's for our new deposit, all in a matter of a day. Somehow it all worked out.

With a moving date set, we had less than one week to get out of Bushwick and into Kensington, and we had to complete the move on one Saturday in early December.

Three Russian teenagers showed up at our front door in the pouring rain, ready to move our stuff. They didn't speak much English, and they had dressed from head to toe in black. We were still throwing clothes in garbage bags as the furniture-carrying soldiers loaded everything into the truck, laughing at us each time they passed.

The moving militia wouldn't take the garbage bags due to some kind of corporate rule until Justin offered them a wad of cash. Then they hauled those down the stairs and into the moving truck with the rest of our things.

Within three hours of the onset of our move across the borough of Brooklyn, I stood in the middle of my new apartment surrounded by sopping wet garbage bags, the shiny plastic glistening under the dim light of our new chandelier.

I smiled and did the Brooklyn Shuffle around my living room.

The Notice

The hour-long ride to get to work from Brooklyn to Long Island hadn't really bothered me when I wasn't pregnant. But after I became pregnant, I craved my second and third breakfast in the car. Thoughts of potatoes and bagels with cream cheese and bacon made my mouth water and stomach growl. Every morning, I stopped in the deli attached to the bank—all in the same building as our office—before going to work cutting checks. It was all becoming an easy habit—until one morning when we walked into our tiny office in Jericho, breakfast potatoes in a Styrofoam container clutched in my eager hands, when five somber faces greeted us.

"Good morning!" I said with a smile before I had a good look at the slumped shoulders in the room. I stopped short, just before my desk, and looked at Ann. "What's going on?" I whispered.

"Nobody knows, but Alex wants a mandatory meeting in ten minutes, and it doesn't look good." Ann's face flushed as she shook her head and twisted her hands into knots.

"What do you mean?"

"Something to do with the bank upstairs." Ann looked at me, then my pregnant belly, and turned back to her computer. She scrunched her face into thin lines.

"Everyone . . . come with me to the conference room. I have some . . . news." Alex's stern voice startled me from my thoughts. I turned on my heels, following him and the others to our conference room, which in that moment felt more like a jail cell: no windows, a clock behind bars, hotter than an oven. We filed in, took our seats, and stared in silence at Alex. We were on trial for our death penalty. I watched the seconds tick by on the clock above our heads before Alex cleared his throat.

"So," he said and wiped beads of sweat from his red forehead. "Our client upstairs is in some serious trouble." He paused and tried to collect himself. Alex was normally a strong and abrasive man, so I wasn't used to seeing this side of him. He looked right at me, almost apologizing with his big mean eyebrows. "That is bad news for all of us, because we aren't sure . . . we aren't sure if we can afford to keep you all employed."

At that point I looked around the office at the staff that had all been there much longer than Justin and me. I started to understand the gravity of this news. We were expecting a baby in the most expensive city in the United States, *and* we were both about to get laid off simultaneously. My mouth went dry.

"Shit," I whispered, and Justin grabbed my knee under the table.

⮑

The official news about the future of our little law office didn't come right away, and for a while everyone seemed to go on with business as if nothing had happened. The bank continued to make loans, the title company continued to produce title documents, and we continued to conduct real estate closings. It was strange how there was a big meeting, then for months everyone acted like it never happened.

We knew better.

Justin applied to every real estate firm in the city, but there was no hope for me. No one would hire a visibly pregnant woman, only to watch her take maternity leave and never return.

When the bank did close, in January of 2010, Alex convinced the main office in Manhattan to transfer us there. Ann and Lee came with us, but Alex and Timothy stayed in Long Island to handle the couple of clients who remained.

Working in the city turned out to be fun. The other girls in the office had an established camaraderie, but they welcomed me. They were the first girls I'd found to talk to who were my own age and not raging drunks or druggies.

Though the office was much bigger, my cubicle was small and consisted only of an old white monitor and keyboard, dangling electrical cords, a wastepaper basket, and a burgundy rolling office chair. The whole office was filled with fifty of these cubicles, and the perimeter of the floor was lined with large, oaky private offices for the partners. I didn't bother to hang photos or personal memorabilia, because I knew I wasn't coming back after maternity leave.

I was always hitting the soft spot on my knee on some kind of jagged screw under the desk. It made me cringe in pain every time. After the third bang, most people would've learned to steer clear. Not me. Regardless, I had a desk, and I had a job. That's all that mattered.

The subway station was close to the office, and there was a great little breakfast shop with the best bagels at the end of the block. Life was good! I fit in well with the fast-moving, focused people. I learned right away when to keep up with the pace or move to the side.

The city office already had a loan funder, so my position was created for me by the managing partner. I scanned old files and labeled them in folders online. Easy peasy.

Justin shared an actual office with another young attorney. They became friends. Justin became involved with more advanced legal proceedings and seemed happy. I liked not having Alex breathing fire down my back. Instead, our managing attorney, Nate, was a quiet man who made his rounds throughout the office each morning to say hello. He promised he had an open-door policy. I liked Nate. He was nice.

After working in the New York City office for only two weeks, another firm offered Justin a job with better pay, closer to home. The new office was just off Wall Street, which would be a much shorter commute compared to our current office past Times Square. Fewer subway transfers and less time on the train meant more time with our baby whenever she arrived.

Justin put in his notice at our current law firm, and right away the boss requested a meeting with him. He asked me to join too. My feet stuck to the insides of my flats with stress sweat. I was six months pregnant, past the cute phase and very uncomfortable. I knocked on Nate's closed door, then opened it. Expensive cologne overwhelmed my nose, and I thought I might hurl.

"Come in, Danielle. Sit down," said Nate. Justin had already picked the chair closest to the window. He smiled, and I sat beside him, closer to the door.

I looked around Nate's office, which was relatively bare besides his law books and various awards and plaques.

"You've both been at the city office for just over two weeks."

"That's right," said Justin.

"So why are you leaving?" Nate asked.

"My family is growing, sir, and I needed to find work." Justin's face was still and confident.

I pulled my dress shirt over my large belly and cleared the nerves from my throat.

"Going to that firm on Wall Street is like jumping from frying pan to frying pan," said Nate, adjusting his tie.

"That may be so." Justin folded his hands in his lap.

"You won't be any happier." Nate scratched his cheek. It reminded me of when Justin had once told me that the higher a person's hand is on his face, the bigger the lie.

"I understand that," said Justin. He sat so still with an unwavering stare. I, on the other hand, couldn't stop shifting in my seat.

I wondered why Nate invited me to this private meeting between the two of them. The heat from the radiator moved over my skin and strangled me into silence. And I suddenly had to pee.

"Unfortunately, this situation is somewhat of a package deal." Nate clasped his hands together and placed the tips of his two index fingers against the spot between his lower lip and chin. He leaned back in his big ugly chair and observed our reactions. A smile of satisfaction curled across his face like a snake. I almost cried. Nate wasn't nice at all. I had been so wrong about him.

"Not sure I understand, sir." Justin leaned forward two inches.

"When we found out the Jericho office was closing, we brought you both on because of your . . . situation."

Justin said, "Ah."

"So, you see my predicament, then?"

"Yes. Yes." Justin flattened out his tie. Slow. Precise.

"Crap," I whispered when I realized.

Justin placed a hand on my knee to shush me. "May I be candid?"

"Of course. Say what you'd like," said Nate.

"It sounds like you're about to let my pregnant wife go for no reason."

Nate pursed his lips and squinted his eyes. I think he was considering his words.

"Is that what you're saying?" Justin leaned in more.

My boss tugged at his collar to let in some air. "No. That's not what I *said*. It's just an inconvenience to keep her on. We have enough parale-gals, so it's extra work for me to find things for Danielle to do." He fum-bled, backpedaled, and jumbled his words together.

"Firing her because I quit would be a bad idea. You don't want to be *that* guy. Trust me."

"Trust me, I'm not letting her go." Nate was a weasel.

"Good. You have my notice. Are we done here?"

"We're done." Nate motioned toward his office door and looked down, busying himself with the paper on his desk.

I stood and glued my eyes to the floor. If I turned my gaze toward Nate, I'd cry. Instead, I offered a half-wave, and waddled to the lady's room.

Toes in the Sand

"**W**hat do you want to do while you're visiting?" I asked Mom. She had flown into Brooklyn from Toledo for the birth of my daughter, Morgan. It was her first trip to New York, more than one year after we'd moved there. Up until her visit, we communicated mostly through vague phone calls—beating around her sickness and the distance between us, but never really facing either of them head-on.

"Nothing, really. I'm just happy to be here." She shrugged and sat on the edge of a barstool, half in our kitchen and half in the living room. New wrinkles rested across Mom's ashen face, and she seemed more fragile than before. Her hair had thinned a bit, and her long nails were unpainted. Everything about her seemed brittle.

"Come on, Mom. You're in New York. We can do whatever you want," I pleaded.

Her eyes sparkled a bit as she pursed her lips. "Well, if you insist . . . I think I'd like to put my toes in the sand and hear a real New York accent."

Justin and I laughed. "Anything else?" I asked.

"Nope. Don't think so." She shrugged and smiled, pushing her glasses back into place.

The next day, we took the F train to Coney Island. It was two days before my due date, and I was a sore and bulging whale, but I'd never been more excited to go to the beach. I knew if she could only see what I saw in New York, then maybe she wouldn't be heartbroken about me living so far away from Toledo.

Between my pregnancy and her cancer, the distance between Mom and me was hard. Justin and I had pretended Mom wasn't sick for so long that we'd started to believe it. After all, it was easy to ignore from six hundred miles away. And if I accepted that she was sick, I'd also have to accept that one day she would no longer be living—that she'd leave my daughter without a grandmother. I couldn't accept that.

When we stepped off the F train, two men greeted us by pounding a rhythm on buckets with drumsticks. Mom wanted to watch, so we stopped in the middle of the tidal wave of commuters, forcing them to part around us like the Red Sea. The drummers pounded, tapped, and twirled their drumsticks in precise unison.

I looked over at Mom as she snapped and danced. "This is so neat, Danielle. They're so good. Stuff like this doesn't exist in Ohio." She put a dollar in the hat in front of the drummers, and they both smiled and offered her a seated bow. She winked at them, always a flirt.

Afterward, I pulled her hand toward the station exit.

Outside, we walked toward the iconic yellow and green Nathan's Hot Dog stand. The smells of meat and onions filled the surrounding air. Crowds of people stood in line beneath the awning, waiting for hot dogs, chili fries, and crisp drinks.

"I'm getting a beer. Want anything?" asked Justin.

"Ooh. I'll take a pop," said Mom.

"It's called soda here, Mom," I corrected.

"So-da! My first piece of New York lingo!" She grinned, and we all laughed.

"I'll get you a Coke," said Justin.

We stood in line, listening to the sharp accents of New Yorkers around us. Their voices blended with all the other accents and languages, creating a sound that I can associate only with New York. In no other city does that blending of cultures happen so seamlessly and beautifully.

Once we reached the awning, we could see the cashiers dressed in yellow and green, taking orders and payment, then turning to fill trays with hot dogs and large cups of beer and soda. The sizzle of food frying, ticking of receipts printing, and the blare of parents yelling at children completed the cacophony.

After Justin ordered and paid, the Nathan's employee handed Mom her soda and said, "Yeh soda," then nodded.

"I love this place already," Mom said.

"But we haven't even made it to the beach yet." I pulled her arm again and guided her toward the boardwalk. Warm, salty air whipped from the ocean, tossing Mom's hair around. Red and blue umbrellas lined the sand in front of us, and a reggae band played music on the boardwalk to our left. Three large, neon, jellyfish-shaped kites danced over the water, rippling with the breeze.

"Come on!" Mom said. This time, she dragged *me* by the hand.

"Where are we going?" I asked.

"You'll see." She pulled me down the steps and onto the sand. "Take your shoes off." She pointed to my feet and tossed her flip-flops next to her in the sand. Then she wiggled her toes around and grinned like a child for the second time.

I rolled my eyes and held her shoulder for balance as I tried to bend over my stomach and pull off my sandals. The sand was hot and littered with bottle caps and cigarette butts.

"Now close your eyes and listen," Mom commanded after my shoes were both upside-down in the sand.

"Listen to what?"

"The waves. The people. The music."

"Okay." I listened.

"Now wiggle the sand between your toes."

I opened my eyes to look at my feet, but my protruding stomach hid them. "It feels dirty."

"Danielle, could you just for once listen to your mother?"

"Sorry." I shut my eyes again and wiggled.

"Feel. It's important to slow down and appreciate the little things. Remember that."

I opened my eyes and looked at her ear-to-ear smile. "Do you like it here?" I asked.

Her smile faded. "It's neat."

"Do you understand now?"

"I do, but that doesn't change me missing you."

Only the Beginning

"**P**ush!"

It had been hours since the bright hospital lights had dimmed to a soft glow. The blinds on the large window to my right were closed, but I knew it was dark. I'd been in that room since the morning. I squinted at the clock. *Nine at night.*

"Push! Push!" the nurses shouted.

My torso burned. My eyesight blurred. I had gone nearly a full day without a single bite to eat, and my body was done.

"You can do this," Justin said. Machines beeped in my ears. All the commotion distracted me, but Justin wouldn't let me give up. I bit the inside of my cheek and concentrated on delivering my little girl.

Throughout my delivery complications, I had gained an audience of nurses and students. At least seven of them, in turquoise scrubs and holding clipboards, surrounded me like I was their lesson. I pushed for two hours in front of my crowd without success. If I failed, all these strangers would witness it.

"Push!" the nurses shouted again.

An epidural kept my body numb from the waist to my toes, but it was too strong. I couldn't feel the urge to push like I was supposed to. I couldn't even feel the softball-sized head squeezing its way through my vagina.

My daughter's heart rate slipped, and the staff went into fast-forward motion. "She's not getting enough oxygen," a nurse shouted, forcing an oxygen mask onto my face. My breath no longer reached the deepest part of my lungs; it thinned, coming in sharp wisps. Sleep beckoned.

"Focus," said the doctor.

"I can't do it anymore," I said. "I'm tired."

"You have to," said Justin. His grip on my hand tightened, and his searing green eyes met mine.

I turned my focus to Mom. She sat in silence on the couch on the side of the room. I peered into her eyes, narrowed in concern. Her hands clutched the strap of her purse, wringing it like a wet washcloth. Though her entire body was tensed, the rest of her face was calm and determined. I pushed again, but nothing.

"She's getting stuck in the birth canal," said the doctor. "We have to give you an episiotomy." I had listened to the lecture on episiotomies in my birthing class. No one wanted them, but it meant they had no other choice to get my child out.

"Whatever we need to do," my husband said. Each syllable rolled off his tongue with perfect timing. He always had the calm and confidence to handle sticky situations with finesse.

Instead of calm, my patience had diminished. "I don't give a shit what you do. Get her out," I said. My voice sounded unfamiliar, weighted down by a concoction of drugs, but fired up with a new willingness to do anything for my daughter.

Thirteen hours after they had admitted me to the maternity ward and minutes after the incision, I pushed twice more, gritting my teeth and letting out a low, primal growl.

My daughter emerged.

I laid my head back and exhaled the breath stuck at the bottom of my lungs. The room erupted with excited hollers, but it lasted only a moment. After that spurt of joy came silence. The room was suddenly so quiet, the lack of sound stung my ears. I lifted my head from the pillow.

"What's wrong?" I whispered. "Is she okay?" I wrestled with the oxygen mask, which was poking me in the eyes and scratching my skin. The room twisted around me like a nightmare. My vision doubled from the loss of blood during delivery. I closed my eyes, opened my eyes. I couldn't focus. "What's happening?" I asked while trying to catch my breath. No one noticed me calling out questions.

But I noticed her.

My child's health became the focus of the room. The umbilical cord strangled her neck. Her arms dangled, and her skin had tinged the color of stone.

She was supposed to cry. That's what they always say. Babies are supposed to cry when they are born. They come out pink and furious. With the cord clinging to her throat like a noose, she did nothing. She didn't scream. She didn't whimper. She didn't even open her mouth and try.

My baby was dying, and it was my fault.

Her silence deafened me. It was acid burning my eardrums. The doctor cut the cord from my body, not my husband who had asked to do it, and took the baby to a small exam table. Nurses hurried to surround her. *What did I do wrong?*

I waited for someone to give me my baby. I was supposed to kiss her, to smell her, to touch her tiny, soft hands and promise that I'd keep her safe.

She needed me.

Nurses cleaned her, weighed her, and took her temperature. I clenched the bed sheets and waited for something, anything, to happen. They rubbed her vigorously with baby blankets and latex-covered skin until garbled sounds erupted from her body. Inch by inch, she turned from blue to pink.

With a sudden fierceness, she shrieked.

I covered my mouth with a trembling hand and cried.

I needed her. I reached both hands toward her, but the nurses didn't look at me.

Instead, they put her in a plastic bed, wheeled her out of the room, and stole that important bonding time from us. *Wait!* I wanted to call out to her, but the drugs, the epidural, the shock, and the lack of sleep strangled my body into stillness.

"What's wrong with her?" Justin asked the doctor, his hand still holding mine. Every fold in his forehead was magnified beneath the soft glow of the nighttime hospital lights. I wished I could feel my legs enough to jump from the bed into his arms, and that I had the strength to speak.

"Your daughter's oxygen levels are low, and she swallowed meconium in the birth canal," the doctor said, bringing his eyes to meet my husband's.

"We're admitting her to the neonatal intensive care unit. They'll keep her safe. I promise she's with the best nurses in the state." He peeled a surgical glove from his fingers and shook my husband's hand. "You can see her tomorrow."

The series of events unfolding around me seemed to be a dream. Nurses had yanked the tiny person I spent ten months holding and protecting in my belly, beneath my skin, away from me without a word. It made no sense. I'd had a picture-perfect pregnancy. Not one issue. Delivery should've been easy.

I stayed there, motionless and muffled, as the doctor and nurses sutured my episiotomy and internal gashes. None of my injuries mattered. I only thought of my child and when I'd be able to see her again.

After a nurse tied the last of my stitches, she helped me walk to a wheelchair and pushed me to my recovery room. I ate a turkey sandwich Justin bought out of a vending machine, because the cafeteria was closed for the night. It had no mustard or mayo, and the starchy white bread stuck to the insides of my throat with each bite. I ate it anyway.

"Are you sure you're okay if I leave?" Justin asked.

"I'm positive." I lied between bites. "One of us needs a good night's sleep. Plus you need to check on the dog."

"You did a great job," Mom whispered into my ear, then pecked my temple.

"Thanks, Mom. Love you guys. Now go before I change my mind and make you sleep in here with me."

"Okay. Love you too." They each gave me one last hug before going back to Brooklyn, an hour away from me in Mineola, Long Island. The doctor and nurses all left at one in the morning, relieved by a crisp, new staff. My daughter stayed in another ward at the other end of the hospital, and for the first time in as long as I could remember, I was completely alone. In my exhausted state, a sense of abandonment overwhelmed me.

After my stomach felt full of old bread, dry turkey, and wilted lettuce, I took the two chalky pills—one for sleeping and one for pain—from the little white cup on my tray and swallowed them with a sip of warm water.

I turned out my light. A ticking clock, a buzzing EXIT sign outside my room, and faint voices echoing from the nurse's station lulled me to sleep.

↢

The next morning, and what felt like an eternity later, with Justin back at my side, I held my pink, pudgy daughter.

I fed her. I changed her tiny diapers and clothes. I watched her open and close her fingers around my thumb. I kissed her and smelled her, understanding how easily everything could have been ripped away forever. "I'll do anything for you, kiddo," I whispered.

I listened to her sucking, smacking, and gurgling, and I welcomed the sound of her determined cry as it sliced through the room. My life, like my daughter's, was only just beginning.

Presence: Part III

A few months after my daughter was born, I had a sudden desire to reconnect with, and have my daughter know, Don. I saw my husband, Justin, as a good man and father, and thought there must be some good in my biological dad too. Even though I hadn't talked to him in ten years, I thought he must have wanted to hear from me. I thought he must have wanted to know about his granddaughter.

In one day, I found him on Facebook. I typed a quick message, asking if he had a daughter named Danielle.

Six months later, he responded, asking me to call right away. But my memories of our last two interactions, and his delay in responding, made me cautious.

Because of how quickly he'd appeared and disappeared out of my life, I didn't call like he insisted. Instead, I typed casual questions about Tennessee and his job. He immediately asked for my address so he could send the baby presents. I messaged him back saying he could mail presents to Mom's house if he insisted on buying her something.

Why didn't he understand that after all those years, I still didn't want his gifts? I wanted more than that, and somehow less than that at the same time: his presence, not his presents.

Still, I had a primal urge to hear everything about him I didn't know. I wanted him to share stories about his love with Mom, their relationship in the beginning, and the hope they shared. I needed to hear things from his perspective about my young, rambunctious mother raising little me.

I reached out to him again on Facebook and wrote, "I was hoping when you had the chance, you could fill in some of the blanks about your relationship with Mom."

He responded with, "It would be better if you called me."

My desperation for something tangible—a story, a shared memory, a smile—all overwhelmed me to the point of confusion. I called him.

"Hello?" he answered.

"Don?"

"That's me."

"Wow. It's strange to hear your voice."

"Why's that?" he said, on edge.

"Dunno. Just is."

"You sure you wanna know about your ma? It ain't good."

"I'm sure you have good stories to share." I checked the monitor; the baby was still resting soundly.

"Well, for starters, your adulterous mother tricked me into having you. And she started seeing Jim before our divorce was finalized," he said.

"Wha—?" His words tripped me up. I had expected . . . something else.

"It's the truth," he said.

"You're lying." My head rang. Tears fell. My anger and my desperation for my biological father to show some kindness welled up inside me. Something in me cracked. Emotions exploded. "I know the truth."

"The hell you do! You've been brainwashed by a pack of liars."

"How can you say such awful things?" Up until that point, I had blamed myself. I'd thought there must have been something wrong with me, otherwise Don would love me. But it wasn't me. Don had so much animosity piled into his heart—had such a wall built up around his emotions.

"Whatever. You're a stupid bitch, just like your mother."

I slammed the phone on the counter and punched the end button with my thumb, gasping for air.

Don was my biological father, but he wasn't capable of being my dad. Not then, not ever.

Last Visit

Justin and I had just driven back from a family ski vacation in lower Vermont. Snow-covered hills and large lodges nestled into the valley provided the perfect backdrop for our quick three-night trip. Inside the lodge, families collected around the fire, drinking cocoa and coffee to warm up. Clumps of boots, wet coats, and gloves were piled up in corners. It was the first time I'd ever been that far north, seen mountains that big. It was only my second time skiing, but I knew I had found a long-term hobby we could do as a family. I called Mom, excited to give her all the details.

"Hey, Mom," I said when she answered.

"Hey." Her voice was flat and distant.

"What's wrong?" I asked.

She cleared her throat, and I unwrapped the scarf from my neck, then slipped out of my snow boots by stepping on each ankle with the opposite foot.

"I went to the doctor today, Danielle. It was a routine scan ..."

"What is it?" I asked. *Déjà vu.*

"There's this thin lining in your stomach, called the visceral peritoneum. The cancer spread there."

"What does that mean? I don't understand what you're saying." *More cancer?* I paced from my living room to my kitchen, ten paces back and forth.

"I don't know. I feel the same, though, and that's all that matters," she replied.

"What did the doctors say?" I asked, pulling on small strands of my hair, twisting it nervously.

"Just worry about you. Worry about you, Justin, and Morgan. Your family, okay?"

"But *you* are my family," I said.

She took a long inhale off a cigarette. "Love you, Danielle. I'll call soon when I find out more."

"Love you too." *Click.* She hung up without saying goodbye.

I called Justin's mom, Petra, in tears because I didn't know what else to do. Petra's mother had suffered and died from colon cancer long before. She understood the disease better than anyone else I knew. I sat down on the kitchen floor. Roxy curled up in my lap.

"Go visit your mom," Petra said.

⸾

I pulled the car into the crumbling driveway back on Custer drive, six hundred miles from my home in Brooklyn, and I sat there. After I'd taken two planes and one rental car, after I'd spent an entire day traveling, I couldn't find the courage to go any farther. *What if it's not like the last time I visited? What if it's worse?* Justin, Morgan, and had I visited to celebrate Mother's Day the year prior. Mom had pretended to be okay. But on the last day, she doubled over in stomach pain, unable to get off the living room chair to hug us. The cancer inside was devouring her bit by bit.

Back on the driveway, I turned to my almost-two-year-old Morgan, buckled into the car seat we'd borrowed from a local friend for this unexpected trip. She smiled at me.

"We're here!" I said. "You get to see Gigi!"

I unbuckled myself, then climbed out and unlatched her. New cracks in the driveway were proof of the harsh winter and my parents' lack of income. There hadn't been enough money to go around ever since Mom had to stop working.

I hesitated before walking up to Mom's back door, unsure of what I'd find inside. My thoughts drifted to the last Thanksgiving we'd visited for. I had been newly pregnant then, and Mom's health had made an unexpected upswing. A turkey stuffed with carrots, celery, and seasoned bread crisped in the oven. Twelve of us had piled into my parents' country kitchen.

Eventually, I found the courage and went inside.

"We're here!" I feigned excitement and walked around the corner of the mudroom and into the family room. Baskets of laundry sat strewn about on the floor. Piles of dog hair and dust accumulated in corners. Stale smoke hovered in the air. Mom sat on the couch, tired and disheveled, still in pajamas even though it was after lunch.

"Hi, Pumpkin." She didn't stand to greet me, so I went to her, setting Morgan down on the rug with one of her toys. Hot tears burned my eyes while hugging my mom's body, which was smaller than it had been when I'd last seen her. When I let go of her, I pushed a short strand of unwashed hair from her face. Her olive skin had paled even more since the last time I'd seen her, eight months prior.

We stayed there for a little while and caught up before I cleaned her house. I needed to make up for lost time, and washing the dishes seemed like a good place to start. I folded her laundry, scrubbed the toilets, vacuumed, mopped, and cooked a simple supper of spaghetti.

Every time Mom got close to Morgan, Morgan cried. She didn't remember Mom.

"She won't look at me," she said.

"Don't worry, Mom. She'll warm up," I said. Morgan didn't.

⤿

The following day, we stopped in to see her oncologist. He notified us that because of the new cancer, Mom wouldn't qualify for any new drug trials. The jerk had given up on her.

We left the doctor's office and sat in silence, listening to the rhythmic pounding of the rain against the windshield of my jellybean-shaped rental car.

Wipers swished, shaking our seats while we waited for the traffic light that had just turned red.

I looked over to Mom. Her fingers lay folded in her lap. My grandmother used to sit that way: proper and poised, hiding the pain. Mom's nails weren't filed and painted like they'd been every day during my childhood. Instead, they were short and natural. Everything about her was different: less meat on her bones, more wrinkles on her face.

"What do you want to do next?" I asked.

She twirled and twisted her gold rings. "I think I'd just like to go home now." She stared out the window, eyes blank.

I glanced back at my sleeping daughter. Morgan didn't understand how sick her grandmother was. She didn't know this could be the last time she'd ever see her alive, hear her voice, feel her hug. How could she?

Mom's newest accessory, a shiny aluminum cane, also lay wedged in the backseat. She had slipped and fallen in the kitchen the week before, breaking a brittle bone in her foot. Chemotherapy had struck again. I couldn't help but wonder how little time we had left together.

"Mom, we're only here for two days. Let's do something fun."

"I don't feel like doing much of anything. I'm tired."

"Well, wake up. We can do whatever you want. Go wherever you want." As soon as the words left my mouth, I knew they had been insensitive and naïve. But cancer had affected me too, yanking me from my twenties and dropping me back into my childhood. I couldn't stop myself.

"I want to rest."

"Rest later." Frustration boiled up like lava. More than anything else in the world, I wanted my mom back: the one who would drop anything for an impromptu dance party; the one who loved to bargain shop at the dollar stores and thrift shops; the one who would laugh at my stupid jokes and promise me the moon. I wanted the mom who wasn't sick.

"I don't want to do anything else right now."

"Stop it, Mom."

"Stop what?"

"Stop acting like you're dying, because you're not!" I gripped the steering wheel so tight the sensation in my fingers faded to a tingle. "You're still alive, and I'm here with your granddaughter." I fought off tears and begged, "Please. Let's do something together."

Mom's breath caught in her throat, and she gasped for air. She hid her face behind her hands and sobbed.

"Mom?" I asked, taking her hand in mine. Someone behind me honked because the light had turned green. Reluctantly, I let go, putting my hand on the wheel and my foot on the gas.

Without looking at me, she said, "I'm not ready to die, but I'm tired of fighting to live."

When Love Sticks Around

I had only been back in Brooklyn for one month when I got the phone call to come home and say goodbye to Mom. Three years of chemotherapy hadn't been able to stop the evil disease inside her from spreading. I remember frantic flight reservations and a red-eye blur of travelers at LaGuardia. Brittany picked me up in Detroit, and I remember nothing of our conversation. I was in shock. Mom wasn't allowed to leave us yet.

In Toledo, I watched her disintegrate for seven days, as I survived mostly on burnt waiting-room coffee. I knew the layout of her white-washed room, the location of the rubber gloves, the information on her whiteboard. I memorized every inch as I watched people come and go with pity filling the wrinkles on their faces. I barely slept. After a week of waiting for something, anything, to happen, my stepfather asked me to go out to eat with him.

"I don't know," I said. "I don't have much of an appetite."

"You gotta eat, Danielle. It's nothing fancy. Just food."

"Fine," I agreed.

Jim moved motorcycle parts and tools aside so I could fit in his truck. I looked over to him, humming along to Queen on the radio, and I struggled to find any words to say. Throughout the years, we'd had very few father-daughter moments. Voicing love and affection never came easy for him.

Living six hundred miles away for the better part of Mom's illness hadn't helped either. Jim and I never spoke on the phone and only saw each other on a few holidays each year. We were nearly strangers.

Without any conversation, he drove me to a hot dog spot where he and Mom had taken Brittany and me as kids.

The restaurant was the same as I remembered. It smelled like a mix of steamed meat byproduct, bad perfume, and stale cigarette smoke. Faux wood booths and brown plastic chairs lined the perimeter and made rows through the restaurant. In the chaos of my life turning upside down, it comforted me to know at least some things never change.

"Tell me the story of how you met Mom." I bit into my chili dog, and a bit of grease dribbled onto my chin.

Jim belched. "Okay. Well, let me think." He sipped his Cherry Coke and wiped his hands on a napkin before continuing. "I met her in a bar and offered to pay for her divorce from your dad."

"Dad!" I slapped his arm playfully. "So, did she take your money?" I asked.

"No." He laughed, and his eyes twinkled. "But she did take a napkin with my phone number on it." I think Jim was the motorcycle-riding, guitar-playing, attention-giving guy Mom needed after my biological father had neglected her.

I looked down at Jim's hands, remembering when he used to sing "My Ding-a-Ling" on the guitar while I shouted the lyrics. I'd had no idea the song was inappropriate at the time. I noticed how his fingers were still calloused from the concrete he'd poured, boats he'd repaired, and elevators he'd built to keep food in the fridge over the years. As a child, I only noticed the smell of his greasy shirts, the lack of fancy labels on my shoes, and the pants that never quite reached my ankles.

"We were pretty poor, weren't we?" I asked.

"Yeah, but we managed most years."

I thought about the time Jim rented out our house while we lived in my grandparents' duplex downtown, so Mom could care for my sick grandpa. I remembered the smell of river water and the sound of beater cars trudging along while I played on the front porch. Mom's belly was round, full of baby, and she had a simple gold ring on her finger.

"I was so mad the day you guys got married," I said.

"Yeah, because you missed some kinda cartoon."

"I was only six." I chewed on an onion ring and sipped my soda. "And

I don't think I understood what was happening."

"Speaking of weddings, I'm still paying yours off," Jim said, shaking his head. "It was so damn expensive."

"I'm sorry." I'd found out a few years earlier about the extra mortgage my parents had added to the house. It had been the only way they could afford my wedding. "It was a beautiful wedding, though."

"Better have been," said Jim. When Justin had asked me to marry him, I knew immediately I didn't want my real father walking me down the aisle. It was Jim who had taught me how to ride my banana-seated bike. It was Jim who had carried me into the hospital to fix my burned hands. And it was Jim who had taught me how to make his world-famous egg salad, still the best I've ever tasted.

"It was. And you were so handsome in that rented tux," I joked.

"Thanks." Jim laughed.

When we'd moved back home after my grandpa's passing, Jim had started changing the house to meet the needs of our family. He first remodeled the front and ripped up a stoop to pour a concrete porch that spanned the width of the house. Then he completed a kitchen remodel with my aunt's throwaway cabinets. But his biggest remodel had been a two-story addition on the back of the house. As a child, I hadn't seen any of that work as a good thing. I only saw the power tools on the kitchen counter as clutter. I only felt the dusty plywood floors beneath my feet as dirty.

If Jim had a sliver of spare time, he spent it rebuilding classic cars in the garage, or commanding the television from the recliner after a long day. I thought it was his way of avoiding me.

But that day I saw something different in Jim. Instead of the grumpy guy from the garage, I saw the man my mom had fallen in love with—the charismatic, funny, eager-to-please man she'd spent the better part of twenty years with.

Maybe Jim hadn't gone out seeking me and my mom when he went to the bar that night. It would have been just as easy for him to walk away when she told him she was separated from her spouse with a young child at home. He could've walked away when their financial situation teetered on the edge of poverty, when my grandfather became sick, or even when my sister was conceived.

I was grateful he'd stuck around.

Fragile Things

In 2012, the day Mom came off the ventilator, I visited her in the ICU. The whiteness of her sterile room made bile rise to my throat. Someone had turned on every light, making the space too bright. Her unwashed, thinning hair had matted against her head. Her eyes had dulled. She had become a vacant shell of the person she once was.

On her tray sat a cup of red Jell-O, foil wrapper neatly secured, spoon still in the cellophane. It reminded me of eating Jell-O as a child.

⤳

Back in 1991, I stood in Mom's kitchen on Custer Drive, making Jell-O with her. The smell of tangy, tart cherries filled the room when Mom ripped the waxy packet open. Red Jell-O was our favorite.

Mom had shoulder-length, permed hair then. She was thin and stylish. I thought she was like a gem, so flawless as she poured the powder into an olive green Tupperware bowl brimming with just the right amount of warm water.

With a cigarette pressed in the corner of her lips and smoke hovering around her face, she whisked and mixed the ingredients together, making metal scratch the plastic. It was the sound of cooking in the kitchen and the sound of love. We added cool water from the tap, whisking some more. I opened the fridge so Mom could move the leftovers to make room.

"Put it in there," said Mom, stamping out her cigarette. I carried the bowl across the kitchen, red liquid sloshing and splashing near the lip.

After the Jell-O was stable on the refrigerator shelf, she closed the door and set the timer for four hours.

But I didn't watch the clock. Instead, I opened the fridge once, twice, three times, checking the consistency.

"Don't rush it," Mom said, pushing her feathered bangs out of her eyes. "It needs time."

⤳

In 1997, on Christmas Eve, my family went to my aunt's house in Michigan. We did this every year. Forty of us arrived in festive red and green clothes. We were a short bunch, but our booming voices made up for it. Mom was chubbier then, with long hair pulled back into a ponytail. She sparkled when she smiled.

Adults took turns at the poker table. Santa stopped by to hand out presents. My aunt forgot the biscuits in the oven, and by the time someone remembered to take them out, their bottoms were burnt.

But it wouldn't have been a party without my aunt's Jell-O jigglers. She filled trays with red squares and stars wiggling in celebration of the day. Sandwiched between the strawberries and seven-layer dip, they were always the first snack on the buffet to disappear.

"Save room!" my aunt shouted. "It's almost time for turkey."

But it was Jell-O we looked forward to, gobbling it up between hide-and-seek and card games, even before turkey, sweet potatoes, salad, and scorched biscuits.

⤳

"Where's my Morgan?" Mom asked, back in the ICU. I had left Morgan with Petra because she was too young to see her grandmother so sick. Tears welled in my eyes.

"She couldn't come." I willed her to lift her hand, to peel the wrapper back and take the smallest bite, but she didn't. Instead, Mom turned her gaze toward the clock and watched more time slip away.

⤳

In 1991, four hours had passed since Mom had put the Jell-O in the fridge on Custer Drive.

"It's ready." She smiled, collecting delicate antique bowls from the cupboard, the ones made of pink and green plaster we hardly used because so many had broken over the years. The same ones Grandma used for her pigs in a blanket.

"Grandma's bowls?"

"Why not?" She shrugged. "They're just things. And what's the point of having a thing if you can't use it?" She scooped the cherry Jell-O into the bowls and sprayed each one with a can of Reddi-wip. We carried our bowls into the living room and sat together, thigh to thigh, on the couch in time to watch *Family Matters*. I laughed between nibbles of my wiggly dessert. "These are the most important moments," she said.

"Why?" I asked.

She frowned, thinking. "I think you'll understand when you're older."

I shrugged. "Love you," I said to Mom.

"Love you too." She smiled.

Letting Mom Go

"**H**ave you asked Terry what her wishes are?" the social worker asked, peering at my stepfather, my sister, and me through her bifocals. My whole family had been called to a meeting there in the intensive care unit waiting room, my home for the past two weeks. We sat in a c-shape on our vinyl hospital chairs, the ones I had slept in one night, just to be there with Mom. I hated those chairs.

And I knew. I knew what my mother's wishes were.

"She wants to go to hospice," the social worker continued, then molded her lips into a tight frown. I wondered how many times a day she gave bad news to families. I wondered if it ever got any easier.

"My God," said my aunt, pulling a tissue from her oversized black leather purse. But I understood. Mom was tired.

∽

"Mom?" I asked, walking toward her the night after she'd found out she had cancer. It was the night Justin and I had driven down from Detroit to Toledo to visit her. I'd needed to see Mom to know she was still herself.

She sat alone in the dark, eyes glazed over as she stared at the front yard through the window. Streetlamp light filtered in through the cracks in the Venetian blinds and reflected a ghostly glow on her cheeks. "Mom? You okay?"

She blinked and turned her head to face me. "No, Danielle. I'm not okay, and I won't ever be okay again."

I stood there, unable to speak or move. Fear held me.

Mom lay her cigarette in the ashtray and cupped her hands over her eyes. "I'm so scared."

I exhaled, relaxed my shoulders, and rushed to her side. "Oh, Mom,"

I said. I tried to choose my words with care because I'd never seen her so upset.

"I don't want to die yet." She lit another cigarette, despite the half-burned one smoking in the ashtray.

"Mom, I will not let you die. You have no choice right now. You fight. No matter what."

"But it might not be that easy. The chemo could kill me, I may need operations, and my cancer might be inoperable. Maybe I want to let things take their natural course." She left the cigarette dangling from her mouth to wring her hands, twist her rings.

"Promise me you will fight. If you can't do it for yourself, do it for us. Brittany, Dad, and me. We need you," I pleaded.

After that, we sat in silence. I waited for her answer as she smoked another cigarette. Eventually, she stamped out the butt of her smoke and peered at me with an unreadable expression. "I promise. But make me a promise too."

"What's that?" I asked. I stared at her and waited.

"You have to promise me that when I tell you I am tired, that I've had enough, you will understand and respect that. When I'm ready to stop fighting, please listen and please understand," she said, her voice adamant.

∽

"It's her decision to make," I said as hot tears stung my eyes.

"Danielle, she ain't in the right state of mind to make a decision like that," Jim said, shifting in his seat. "She could get better."

"Dad, Mom doesn't want to die with all those tubes connected to her body. She wants to be comfortable." Admitting she would die out loud shredded my heart to pieces.

"She can die at home," he said. No one else said a word, so he went on, "She can be comfortable there." He raised his hands, slapped his thighs.

"That's not what she wants," I said. I pleaded with him because I knew this was my one chance to fight for her. If I didn't stand my ground, maybe I would regret it for the rest of my life. "We have to let her go, Dad. We have to do what she wants." Inside, bits of myself withered away and disappeared. I died just a little there in that room, to do what I needed to do for Mom.

Jim let out a long, deep sigh, drenched with sadness and defeat. "Well, I don't know. I guess if you kids think that's what's best for your mom . . ." He looked at Brittany, then at me. My eyes filled with fresh tears. I was so terrified of her dying. I exchanged glances with Brittany, so quiet and so distant, her chestnut eyes red and wet.

"It's what she wants, Dad," I repeated.

The next morning, Brittany and I walked side by side behind the two emergency medical transporters who wheeled Mom to the ambulance. I let the tears blind my eyes and trusted my ears to follow the echoes of their shoes. Before we left, they gave Mom an extra dose of morphine for the short drive. Brittany and I rode in the ambulance with her, strapped in the gurney, to her new, and last, home.

At the hospice center, Mom's room had a large patio that overlooked a white gazebo and a small pond. We'd picked the room ourselves, and I hoped she'd love it. The room was much brighter and nicer than the cold, stark room filled with tubes and machines in the ICU. Several windows allowed spring light to reflect off the peach walls and warm her cheeks, maybe reminding her of summer, her favorite season. Only one tube connected to the wall to give her morphine. I knew the doctors would no longer treat Mom's failing liver, her cancer, or any infections. Instead they made her comfortable, so she could rest for the time she had left.

Dance of the Monarchs

In second grade, my teacher brought in small caterpillars for the class to have as pets. We raised them, fed them, and cared for them. After crawling about and munching on leaves for a month, they wrapped themselves into a chrysalis, went through metamorphosis, and turned into butterflies.

On the last day of school, we released them back to nature. My heart broke because I would never again see them. I missed them the second they danced away.

After school, I ran off the bus, down the street, and into Mom's arms. She held me tight. Then she wiped my tears and said, "Oh, sweetie, setting them free was a good thing. Butterflies have to spread their wings and fly. They will never be happy while trapped in a cage."

〜

On Easter Sunday almost two years after my daughter was born, my stepdad woke me from my sister's bed early in the morning, before the sun's fingers had the chance to tap the sky.

"Danielle," he whispered. My eyes flew open, and I looked over to him, already dressed, standing at the door. "It's time," he said.

"Okay, I'll get dressed," I responded, still half asleep. The previous few days had been hard on all of us, and exhaustion had settled over me. As I searched for my wedding ring on Brittany's nightstand, I knocked over two of my beer cans from the night before. I gathered them up, tossed them in the trashcan, and finished getting ready, a feeling of nausea sitting deep in my belly.

I met Jim downstairs. He stood silent, looking past the patio into Mom's small patch of a backyard, dark under the early morning moonlight. I wished he would be a little more open with his feelings.

"Ready?" I asked him as I chewed on an antacid for my stomach.

"Yep. Let's go," he said and handed me a coffee. I followed him to the car, climbed in, and buckled my seatbelt.

Neither Jim nor I said much on our twenty-minute ride. We had already said our goodbyes to Mom two days prior. We gave her permission to go and said we'd be okay without her, even though I didn't fully believe that we would.

It was still dark out when we got to the building, a modern steel and brick façade I'd grown to hate over the last two weeks. I was thankful I didn't have to look at it. We walked through the double glass doors, down the hallway, and into Mom's room, which was also dark. We sat, afraid to say out loud what we all knew.

I sat in a couch across the room from Mom, watching the rise and fall of her chest. The only sound was that of her breath, a gurgle, like she was drowning in her own body.

Once the sun rose, people filtered in. Aunts, uncles, cousins, and friends all came to kiss her goodbye. When Brittany finally got there with her boyfriend, it felt like late morning, but I avoided the clock. Someone brought breakfast sandwiches and coffee. I didn't want food, but I was grateful for the caffeine.

Mom's pastor came and whispered a prayer.

I looked at Brittany. Her eyes were soaked and red.

After the pastor left, and I had expressed my gratitude for all the people who came to show support, I left the room to call Justin and check on Morgan. They were with Justin's family for Easter, states away in Long Island, New York.

"Danielle, you sound exhausted." Justin's voice flooded with worry. "Try to get some rest." My eyes agreed with him, heavy from too many long days, so I took his advice and found a quiet spot on a padded bench in the hallway.

I awoke to someone tapping my shoulder. My eyes flitted open to see one of Jim's friends standing over me. His eyes were wide and red, and before he could say it with words, I knew. I stumbled into her room, where at least twenty faceless people had crowded in silence, and pushed my way through until I was beside Brittany and in front of Mom. Her body was so still. I waited for the rise and fall of her chest—for something, anything, to happen. But it didn't. From the bed in front of me, there was no movement, no gurgle, nothing. Mom had passed away while I'd napped.

Later, when the tears stopped spilling from my eyes, I mopped myself off the floor and went outside to dry my cheeks under the April sun. It was the kind of spring day just warm enough for a light jacket and open windows. Mom loved days like those, where the breeze would toss her hair around, and she could work in her garden without breaking a sweat, or swing on her porch drinking lukewarm coffee.

I turned my focus to Brittany, who had come outside to stand beside me. Her vacant eyes stared into the distance, but she said nothing. I wanted to be strong for her because that's what big sisters are supposed to do, and that's what Mom would have wanted. But I couldn't be strong. Not right then, anyway. I had to give myself space to grieve.

I took a deep breath in through my nose and closed my eyes. The scent of fresh-cut grass and pond water filled my nose. I exhaled and opened my eyes to see Jim walking toward us. A large Monarch butterfly danced around his head before it soared toward the sky.

Who Will Wear Her Reading Glasses?

Mom had been gone for three days before I realized that no one would wear her reading glasses ever again. She would no longer push them up her nose, past the place they were meant to sit, as she crocheted a scarf or painted a plaster figurine with her steady nurse's hand. They would no longer slide off her face as she fell asleep reading a Stephen King novel. They wouldn't sit on the top of her head as she squinted to read a text on her phone.

Who will tuck them into their case or let them hang from the purple beaded eyeglass chain that used to dangle from her neck? I wondered. The glasses would no longer sway from the chain as she danced across the living room floor to the Temptations or Whitney Houston. She would no longer bite the plastic earpiece while reminiscing about the patients she once had.

The glasses would no longer travel with Mom to the grocery store and get lost at the bottom of her purse next to the list she swore she left at home. She used to find them there just as she dug around for her wallet at the cash register, causing her to laugh for seemingly no reason.

When I realized this, I fell into my couch and stifled sobs with the throw pillows. Her abandonment of those reading glasses ripped every breath from my lungs. The image of her glasses collecting dust somewhere without an owner emptied out my heart.

The pain was so crushing I thought it might kill me. For days I wouldn't eat, wouldn't get off the couch, wouldn't see through the cloud of tears to understand that life went on. How could it be true, after all? How could life go on without my mom?

But somehow, after months of depression strangling me, tears drowning me, sadness stealing moments from my daughter, I glued fractions of myself together and came out alive and mostly okay. I dusted myself off and put one foot in front of the other, as painful as it was to start. To heal, I started writing about her.

Four years after she passed, I went to Toledo to visit. It wasn't the first time I had visited since she'd passed, but it was the visit with the most clarity. Jim had been working on a kitchen remodel, tearing down walls and cabinets, installing new flooring and light fixtures. Mom's reading glasses, folded on the counter, caught my eye. Someone had placed them in a wooden box next to her address book and the pens. Not much had moved in that spot since the day she'd died.

I wiped the glasses clean with my thumbs; I couldn't believe that the lenses were still in perfect condition. Jim had to have forgotten they were there. Maybe he wasn't attached to them like I was. I examined the wire rims, remembering how she used to tilt her head up to keep them from falling down her nose. She never went to the eye doctor and always bought her glasses from the Dollar Store. She would say, "They're just as good, and they only cost me a dollar." Mom was a bargain shopper, even until the end.

I put them on my face, just to try them. Everything around me lost its focus and blurred. I blinked, and my eyes watered. I blinked again, and a headache set in. The glasses made me dizzy, so I removed them from my face and folded them into my palm.

"Can I keep these?" I asked Jim.

He belched with a pencil in his mouth, taking it out to say, "Danielle, I don't care about those old things." He put the pencil back in his mouth and went back to measuring.

I returned the glasses to their plastic case, which I found in the cabinet beneath the pens and address book, and I dropped them inside my purse. At home, I put them into a small box with Grandma's pearl-dotted gloves that she'd worn while grocery shopping, and Grandpa's white handkerchief he'd kept in his shirt pocket by his ticker.

Corner Hutch

When I was little, before Grandma, Grandpa, or Mom battled sickness, I would stand in front of the brown hutch in Grandma's house in this strange room between the dining room and the living room. Along one side of the room was a large radiator with a cream-colored statue of the Virgin Mary's head sitting on top. Her hands in prayer, she somehow calmed me, even though I was always so sure the tears in her eyes were real. I imagined her coming to life and looking over my grandparents while they were sleeping. Then there was a picture of the Last Supper hanging on the wall, which scared me because everyone in the painting had distant, haunted eyes.

But the hutch, I loved.

Vintage bottles of Avon perfume stayed behind the glass doors like little statues. I didn't have many toys at Grandma's house, so I sometimes would ask her to open the door and let me see the bottles up close. They were each so different: the white cat smiling wide, the dancing girl, and the sitting deer. My favorite was shaped like Betsy Franklin sewing the American flag. Each bottle smelled the same, like fields of potent flowers drudged in a sea of harsh chemicals.

The hutch was stained dark then, and I remember it being much sturdier.

When Grandma moved in with us after Grandpa passed away, she brought little to our house: only her blue velvet rocking chair, her Elvis clock with the swinging hips, and the hutch.

Mom used the hutch to house tiny tea sets she collected. I don't know what happened to all the perfumes, but I often imagine them on display at Goodwill or in a flea market somewhere, waiting for a new owner.

No one had paid attention to the big brown hutch in our farmhouse dining room. The hideous burgundy wallpaper and shelves full of antique mason jars distracted us. But when Brittany was only two, she noticed. She opened the doors and climbed the shelves like a ladder. When she reached the top shelf, the whole hutch came crashing down. She curled into a ball, tucked between two shelves, and came out without a single scratch or bruise. But most of the glass knick-knacks broke, and the hutch hinges seemed weaker and more fragile than before.

Mom liked to refinish things, to make them match whatever decorating mood she was in. I don't think it ever occurred to her to change the color of the hutch until Grandma passed away. In the absence of her mother, Mom painted the hutch a sunny yellow, to remind her of brighter days and maybe Grandma's kitchen on Lagrange Street. After that it was blue for the duck phase, then hunter green, and then burgundy to match her flowery dining room wallpaper. Never once did she sand or scrape away the existing paint. She piled and layered it right on top of the old. In a hurry for change, I suppose.

Brittany and I divided up some of Mom's belongings when she passed away, and I knew I had to have that corner hutch. It had been part of my life since I was born, always looming in the background of my memories. I wanted to experiment with refinishing something. I wanted to bring my Ohio memories home.

Jim complained about hauling it. But he still strapped it to a trailer and drove it through mountains to hand it off to me. Pieces fell off and wood splintered along the back, but it remained intact for the most part.

At first, I hoped to get rid of all the layers and paint it right. I learned the hard way that stripping paint is not a beginner's project. I poured on paint thinner, watched the colors bubble and swell, and scraped it off, only to find more paint hidden beneath. As I sanded, stripped, and sanded more, old colors revealed themselves with more childhood memories. It was like peeling a never-ending onion.

But I didn't give up.

Instead, I stopped at the craft store and picked up some chalk paint, which I'd heard needs little prep work. I am my mother's daughter, after all. I cleaned the paint dust from the hutch and layered on the new paint. Once it was dry, I sanded the edges, giving the whole piece a distressed farmhouse look. I waxed and buffed the hutch and moved it to my computer room.

It now houses my favorite books.

Thank You

I couldn't have written this book about family relationships without my husband and two daughters, who encouraged me every step of the way (even though it wasn't easy). Also, to my mom in heaven, and to Jim, who answered any question I had when my memory got a little fuzzy.

I also couldn't have done this without my online tribe of writing friends. Amy, Margaret (who has since passed away), Melony, Donna-Louise, Hema, Michelle, Tara, and Laura, thank you for reading bad drafts and continuing to encourage me so much along the way.

Then there's my Riverside Writers critique group. Y'all are amazing!

Finally, thank you to my editor and cheerleader, Chelsey Clammer, author of *Circadian* and *Body Home*. Without you, I wouldn't have a thank you note to write. You are the best.

About the Author

Born and raised in Ohio, Danielle Dayney got her start writing rock concert reviews and band interviews for Toledo-based music magazine *The Glass Eye*. After leaving Ohio, she set aside her journals for several years to work in the real estate industry, but after her mother passed away from cancer, she returned to writing, initially as a cathartic way to understand her grief.

Since then, her work has appeared in *The Fredericksburg Literary and Art Review*, online at *Sunlight Press*, *Dead Housekeeping* and *The Mindful Word*, and in several anthologies including *The Virginia Writers Centennial Anthology*, *Nevertheless We Persisted*, *Beach Reads: Lost and Found*, and *Beach Reads: Adrift*. She has also received awards for two creative nonfiction essays at BlogHer.

Danielle lives in the rolling hills of Virginia with her husband, two daughters, and two dogs. Follow her blog at https://danielledayney.com.

CPSIA information can be obtained
at www.ICGtesting.com
Printed in the USA
BVHW062021101121
621198BV00009B/981

9 781953 021199